A Guide to
WORKER PRODUCTIVITY EXPERIMENTS IN THE UNITED STATES 1971-75

by
Raymond A. Katzell
Penney Bienstock
Paul H. Faerstein

New York University

Prepared for
WORK IN AMERICA INSTITUTE, INC.
Scarsdale, New York

New York · New York University Press · 1977

The material in this project was prepared under grant 21-36-75-17 from the Employment and Training Administration, U.S. Department of Labor, under the authority of Title Three, Part B of the Comprehensive Employment and Training Act of 1973. Researchers undertaking such projects under government sponsorship are encouraged to express freely their professional judgement. Therefore, their points of view or opinions stated in this document do not necessarily represent the official position or policy of the Department of Labor.

Library of Congress Catalog Card No. 77-760-42.

ISBN: 0-8147-4566-0 (Case); 0-8147-4567-9 (Paper)

Printed in the United States of America.

First Edition

FOREWORD

The American labor force nears 95 million and is growing. During a period of slowed economic growth and recurring energy crises, the economy has
idle plant capacity and idle workers. Employers are increasingly concerned
about the effective use both of capital and of human resources. Whereas the
application of new and advanced technology is prompted by the profit motives
of the manufacturers and users, there is no parallel market mechanism for
the dissemination of practical ideas to improve the productivity of people
in the workplace.

With, however, the increased quality and growing cost of manpower, employers are more anxious to learn how others have increased worker productivity. In order to advance this knowledge, Work in America Institute
(under a grant from the Department of Labor, Education and Training Administration) commissioned this unique <u>Guide to Worker Productivity Experiments
in the United States</u>.

The objective of this original <u>Guide</u> is to define work structures and
experiments which have improved the quality and quantity of products or services. These comprehensive examples are now available to the universe of
potential employer users. They can imitate or modify the lessons of other
successful employers to fit their own special needs.

As Dr. Raymond Katzell explains in Chapters 1 and 2, the <u>Guide</u> is cross-
indexed and referenced within a useful, schematic framework. Thus, it is
simple to locate the most pertinent cases from among the 103 studies, organized by occupation, industry, or nature of the experimental terms of reference. This meticulous analysis and indexing serves to readily link the
reader's needs to the applicable productivity experiment.

Work in America Institute is pleased to make these productivity experiments available to a wide audience of employers in order to advance productivity and the quality of working life.

Jerome M. Rosow

CONTENTS

SECTION I

INTRODUCTION AND PROCEDURE

CHAPTER 1

OVERVIEW OF CONTENTS AND METHOD

This volume reports the results of a review of recent field experiments aimed at understanding and improving worker productivity. By this we mean changes in the productivity of workers themselves, in terms of their ability or effort, and not changes in the productivity of organizations or industries which may be attributable to technological, political, or economic factors. The present chapter explains the procedure we followed for the review and how its outcomes are organized in the remainder of this document.

The studies covered by the review consist of all those that we could locate that possessed the following characteristics:

1. Each study was published in the United States in publicly available form, typically as journal articles, books or monographs.

2. The date of publication was in the five-year period 1971 to 1975, inclusive; a few studies published in 1976 were included, but in general, the 1976 literature appeared too late to be systematically covered.

3. The study was performed in the United States.

4. The study consisted of an experiment, that is, the planned change of some practice or condition of work. Studies limited to surveys or comparisons of existing practices were excluded.

5. The experiment was conducted in a permanent organization which was established to create or distribute goods or services and in which workers found gainful employment.[1] Included are studies performed in either the private or the public sector, and in profit-making as well as non-profit

---

[1]The terms "worker" or "employee" will be used to refer to all organization members regardless of status or function.

institutions. Excluded are experiments performed in temporary "organizations" under laboratory or simulated conditions.

6. The results of the experiment included some aspect of worker productivity. Productivity was liberally defined to embrace any aspect of
worker-output (such as quantity, quality, or value), or any aspect of input
or cost expended to achieve output (such as labor or material costs, turnover, absenteeism, or accidents). A productivity improvement, therefore,
consisted of an increase in output without a proportional increase in input,
or a decrease in input without a corresponding loss of output. Most studies
reported only changes either in an output or in an input, rather than in
their ratio; these changes in input or in output were assumed, perhaps
erroneously, to reflect productivity changes.

7. In order to permit evaluation, the productivity results had to be
reported in some quantitative form; thus, articles offering impressions
alone did not qualify for inclusion.

8. As we were not content with correlational studies, those that did
no more than to report the validity of some procedure did not qualify; It
was necessary for the study to show by some follow-up that adoption of a new
procedure had or had not affected productivity.

Within the area defined by the above boundaries, we covered all the
studies we could locate both by means of 100% check of certain journals and
by the use of several comprehensive abstracting-and-indexing references.[2]
In short, this document is intended to be an _inclusive_ guide to the literature on worker productivity during 1971-1975, rather than focusing on more
rigorous "prototype" studies, as was done in the policy evaluation recently

[2]Our search system is described in the Appendix.

4

published by the senior author and his associates.[3] The present survey also differs from the other study in that the province of the present survey is productivity; job satisfaction and quality-of-work-life data are cited secondarily if collected in association with productivity results, but are neither necessary nor sufficient to qualify a study for inclusion.[4]

Although the emphasis here is more on bibliographic inclusiveness than on evaluative selectivity, our abstracts nevertheless endeavor to alert the reader to methodological shortcomings or limitations that we believe need to be considered in the drawing of conclusions from each study. This point becomes more apparent in the next part, which outlines the form in which our survey is reported.

Presentation Format

The bibliographical and survey objectives of this report are served by the presentation, in Section II, of a set of short abstracts of each of the

---

[3]Katzell, R.A., Yankelovich, D., et al. Work, productivity and job satisfaction. New York: The Psychological Corporation, 1975.

[4]With respect to the foregoing differences in scope, as well as with respect to differences in time-frame and format, the present survey also differs from these other recent volumes covering related topics:

Glaser, E.M. Improving the quality of worklife ... An in the process, improving productivity. Los Angeles: Human Interaction Research Institute, 1975.

Srivastva, S., et al. Job satisfaction and productivity. Cleveland: Department of Organizational Behavior, Case Western Reserve University, 1975.

Suttle, J.L., van Maanen, J., Schein, E.A., Hackman, J.R., Lawler, E.E., III, Alderfer, C.P. & Strauss, G. Improving life in organizations. Washington, D.C.: U.S. Department of Labor, 1975.

Taylor, J.C., Landy, J., Levine, M. & Kamath, D.R. The quality of working life: An annotated bibliography. Los Angeles: Center for Organizational Studies, University of California, 1973.

studies found to meet the criteria stated above. The abstracts are presented in alphabetical order by surname of (first) author. At the top of each abstract is a coded key giving information about the type of industry studied (according to the United States Department of Commerce Standard Industrial Classification); the type(s) of workers involved (according to the United States Department of Labor Dictionary of Occupational Titles); the nature of the experimental program (e.g., training, management by objectives, etc.); and the productivity measures used to assess results (e.g., quality of production, absenteeism, etc.). Each abstract then lists the following information:

1. Complete references--author(s), title, publisher or journal.
2. Principal conclusions.
3. Name or nature of the organization studied.
4. Characteristics of the workers who were involved.
5. Nature of the experimental program.
6. Method by which it was installed or introduced.
7. Experimental design or method.
8. Productivity results obtained.
9. Other results, if any.
10. Any evidence of intervening factors that may account for the results.
11. Chief limitations or threats to validity of conclusions.

The foregoing features are explained in greater detail in Section II's opening pages, which should be studied before the abstracts are read.

Section III is the Appendix, which details our sources of literature search.

Section IV contains several indexes to assist the reader in locating those abstracts that pertain to a particular subject. The first four indexes

actually comprise a subject index, broken down four ways. The reader interested in locating abstracts dealing with a particular kind of productivity-
improvement program should consult Index A. The reader interested in
studies bearing on a certain aspect of productivity, such as quality of production or turnover, should consult Index B. Index C classifies the
abstracts on the basis of type of worker, and Index D on the basis of type
of organization. Finally, Index E is an author index, by which one may
locate studies authored or co-authored by any given person. A bibliography
is not needed, since the alphabetical arrangement of abstracts in Section II
forms in essence an annotated bibliography.

    Chapter 2, which concludes the present Section, is an integrative
summary of the subject matter contained in the abstracts. This chapter
seeks to give a concise picture of what emerges when one considers as a
whole the 103 reports of experiments on worker productivity published in the
United States during the past five years.

CHAPTER 2

INTEGRATIVE SUMMARY OF RESEARCH

In developing an overview of what has been accomplished in this field over the period under consideration, it probably is most helpful to organize the studies in terms of the nature of programs. These, after all, are the "action levers" or "treatments"--technically, the independent variables--by means of which people have tried to improve worker productivity.

As we surveyed those attempts, it seemed meaningful to classify them into fourteen types, each of which may be thought of as a "program." Inevitably, particular organizations have employed their own form of any given program; but all of those grouped under a given program-rubric have much in common.

In some instances, an experiment may have made several changes, either simultaneously or in succession, which represent more than one type of program. Job redesign, for example, may have been accompanied by changes in the compensation system. Such experiments are considered in connection with each of the several programs that they illustrate.

It may be noted that sometimes the authors of a study have not identified it as incorporating some programmatic feature. In our example, the experiment in job design may have been titled and defined as such, without being referred to as, also, a study of compensation; however, since the compensation system has been modified as well, we cross-listed the experiment both as one in job design and as one in compensation, and we discuss it in both contexts.

In some instances, the experiment has embraced so many different programmatic features as to represent in truth a different socio-technical
system. Such experiments are classified in their own category, as it is
impossible to begin to sort out the several programs' respective contribu-
tions to the observed effects.

The fourteen categories of programs in terms of which the experiments
are considered are as follows, each with its own program code-number:

1. Selection and placement.
2. Job development and promotion. *(Job enrichment)*
3. Training and instruction.
4. Appraisal and feedback.
5. Management by objectives.
6. Goal setting.
7. Financial compensation.
8. Job design.
9. Group design.
10. Supervisory methods.
11. Organizational structure.
12. Physical working conditions. *(Safety)*
13. Work schedule. *(Production, xy)*
14. Socio-technical system.

In summarizing the research on these programs, we present, for each, a
table listing the productivity outcomes measured, the experiments showing an
improvement in terms of those criteria, and those failing to show that
result.

9

The productivity outcomes or criteria are categorized as follows, each with its assigned criterion code number:

Production

1. Quantity or rate of production.

2. Quality or accuracy of production.

3. Financial costs.

4. Miscellaneous.

Withdrawal of Personnel

5. Turnover.

6. Absenteeism.

7. Tardiness.

8. Miscellaneous.

Disruptions

9. Accidents.

10. Strikes.

11. Slowdowns.

12. Grievances.

13. Alcoholism and drug abuse.

14. Miscellaneous.

15. Attitudes (If measured in addition to one of the above.)

For each study tabulated, the type of worker is shown. By a system of letters or asterisks corresponding to a key at the foot of each table, we also show when the effects of the program on some criterion of productivity were mixed; when the statistical significance[5] of the result was not reported or was doubtful; or when the methodological limitations of a study were so severe as, in our judgment, to render the validity of the finding questionable. Regarding the last point, perusal of the abstracts in Section II reveals that, as is to be expected, virtually no experiment was completely unflawed; those noted here as "questionable," however, are those whose fallibility suggests the need for great caution in accepting the result.

Each study listed in the tables and discussed in the text carries an identification number corresponding to its abstract number in Section II, so that it is easy to refer to any abstract for additional information.

Program 1. Selection and Placement

In this category are studies that assessed the consequences of a change in how the organization was staffed (including any of the activities associated with recruitment, selection, and placement).

Table 1 reveals that few studies showing that adoption of a new staffing procedure had affected productivity were published during the period under review. The main productivity target of such studies was turnover. One study (90) showed that careful selection together with training could improve turnover of paraprofessionals. Other studies (20, 100) failed to find any beneficial effects of job-orientation experiences. (It may be noted that this is not consistent with earlier studies showing that turnover of sales personnel may be reduced when they are given realistic job information.)

In line with the current emphasis on affirmative action, one study (52)

---

[5]"Statistical significance" refers to a calculation showing that the odds are less than 1 in 20 that the observed effect was due to chance; in science, those odds are commonly accepted as "significant."

Table 1. Program 1: SELECTION AND PLACEMENT
(numbers refer to abstracts)

Productivity Criterion	Studies Finding Improvement	Studies Not Finding Improvement
Turnover	90 (c) paraprofessionals	20 sewing-machine operators 100 telephone operators
Attitudes	*52 (b) salesmen & repairmen	

*Also found no difference between blacks and whites as far as ratings or programs.
(b)Statistical significance not reported or doubtful.
(c)Questionable because of major limitations of experiment.

in this program category followed up matched black and white sales representatives and equipment repairmen and found no appreciable differences in their subsequent success; however, the small samples involved render that finding merely suggestive.

Program 2. Job Development and Promotion

Strangely enough, with all the attention given to career opportunities and promotion systems, no study was reported in which this type of program was subjected to experimental evaluation. This type of program's representation in the literature under review is as an element in total work-redesign (Program Code 14, below). For instance, a successful systems-redesign in Cryovac Division of W.R. Grace (77) included creation of a new hierarchy of skills through which workers could progress with training. Since career programs as such, however, have not been experimentally evaluated, we present no table corresponding to that rubric.

Program 3. Training and Instruction

As shown by the length of Table 2, various types of training programs continue to represent one of the most common techniques for attempting to improve productive performance of workers. Such programs have been used with success in a variety of settings with many different types and levels of workers. Positive results have been reported in terms of various criteria of productivity, including quantity, quality, and cost of production. However, several orientation or coaching programs for new workers have failed to have hoped-for effects in reducing turnover--possibly because the roots of the problem lie in basic conditions of work or in more inaccessible socio-economic determiners of worker behavior; in short, training may fail when tried as a remedy for the wrong disease.

13

Table 2.   Program 3:   TRAINING AND INSTRUCTION
(numbers refer to abstracts)

Productivity Criterion	Studies Finding Improvement	Studies Not Finding Improvement
Production Quantity	28 supervisors 38 (b,c) supervisors 59 (b) retail-store workers 62 (b,c) supervisors 66 (b) auditors 78 (b) supervisors 79 (b,c) mental-health workers 91 (b,c) factory crews	
Production Quality	6 disadvantaged clerical workers 12 psychiatric aides 17 (b) police 18 (c) nurses 32 managers 38 (b,c) supervisors 65 psychiatric aides 66 (b) auditors 70 psychiatric aides 72 military police **84 disadvantaged workers 87 health aides 92 (b,c) paraprofessionals *drugs*	3 (c) teachers *46 (c) psychiatric residents 67 (b,c) counselors 96 counselors
Production Costs	2 (b) supervisors 13 (b,c) hospital workers 19 managers 59 (b) retail-store workers 91 (b,c) factory crews	
Job Success	4 (c) executives *job - performance rating* 6 disadvantaged workers 82 disadvantaged youth	
Turnover *#84*	13 (b,c) hospital workers 27 disadvantaged workers 82 disadvantaged youth **84 (a,c) disadvantaged workers 90 (c) disadvantaged workers	69 disadvantaged workers 80 disadvantaged workers 83 (a) disadvantaged workers 100 telephone operators

14

Table 2.   Program 3:   TRAINING AND INSTRUCTION (cont'd.)
(numbers refer to abstracts)

Productivity Criterion	Studies Finding Improvement	Studies Not Finding Improvement
Absenteeism #84	2 (b) supervisors 13 (b,c) hospital workers 102 managers	84 (c) disadvantaged workers
Accidents	2 (b) supervisors	
Grievances	2 (b) supervisors	
Disciplinary Actions	2 (b) supervisors	
Attitudes	18 (c) nurses 102 managers	96 counselors

*New training procedure less effective than old.
**One program superior to another.
(a)Results mixed, but generally supporting the inference.
(b)Statistical significance not reported or doubtful.
(c)Questionable because of major limitations of experiment.

The training techniques used have run the gamut from familiar lecture, discussion, and role-playing procedures to newer approaches such as video replay (17, 19) and automated instruction (72). Perhaps the most important new trend involves applications of behavioral psychology, featuring the elements of clarifying desired behavior; providing prompt and specific feedback; and delivering regular positive reinforcement contingent on the trainee's manifestation of desirable behavior. One type of training technique employing these elements is "modeling" in which desirable behavior is communicated through the trainee's witnessing the performance of an influential role-model; this is coupled with verbal reinforcement of the trainee's efforts (see, for example, 28).

Another version of the use of reinforcement is furnished by a management-training program (102): role-playing was linked either with delayed feedback (verbal reinforcement) or with delayed-plus-immediate feedback (verbal reinforcement via earphones); both reinforcement techniques resulted in perceived changes in behavior, as well as in reduced absenteeism of subordinates. A related program (1) focused on improving quality of output: during weekly meetings with operators, foremen gave verbal reinforcements, resulting in overall quality improvements which, if sustained, would result in annual savings of $77,000. Such behavior techniques seem quite promising.

An additional recent area of activity has been the use of training to help disadvantaged workers be productive and successful. Several such experiments have yielded positive results (6, 70, 72, 82, 84, 90).

Finally, it should be noted that not all of the predominantly favorable effects summarized in Table 2 can be credited to training alone. In some instances, training was coupled with one or more other changes in ways that

16

make it impossible to sort out just what cause was responsible for what effect. The abstracts presented in Section II enable the reader to see what specific additional program features, if any, were used in each of the studies listed in Table 2. Nevertheless, the overall impression is that personnel training, when competently applied to situations in which the productivity problem lies largely in the fact that workers have yet to learn effective ways of doing their jobs, can be an effective way of improving productivity.

Program 4. Appraisal and Feedback

As with training, programs in this category are based on the assumption that helping workers to learn how better to do their jobs can improve productivity. Whereas training provides programmed experience for groups of workers, however, the present category consists of procedures for appraising each worker's on-the-job performance and then furnishing individualized guidance via feedback, counseling, or coaching.

Most of the several recent studies contained in Table 3 represent an approach that differs from the old style of performance-appraisal with associated post-appraisal counseling every six or twelve months. The more recent approach is much more focused, specific, and frequent. Performance goals or behavioral objectives are made clear, and each employee's performance is frequently reported back to him or her, typically also with positive reinforcement, such as praise for good performance.

This approach seems to be getting good results in a variety of settings and with various types of workers. One unusual experiment (36) has even shown that feeding back specific results of the ratings given them by their subordinates can improve the performance of supervisors. In addition,

17

Table 3. Program 4: APPRAISAL AND FEEDBACK
(numbers refer to abstracts)

Productivity Criterion	Studies Finding Improvement	Studies Not Finding Improvement
Production Quantity	1 (c) die casters 5 (b,c) various	
Production Quality	18 (a) nurses 36 supervisors 48 blue-collar	1 (c) die casters 67 (b,c) counselors
Production Costs	1 (c) die casters 5 (b,c) various 48 blue-collar	
Turnover		69 various, disadvantaged
Absenteeism		48 blue-collar
Tardiness	21 (b,c) white-collar	
Accidents	48 blue-collar	
Attitudes	18 (a) nurses 48 (a) blue-collar	1 (c) die casters

(a)Results mixed, but generally supporting the inference.
(b)Statistical significance not reported or doubtful.
(c)Questionable because of major limitations of experiment.

feedback has been found to supplement the positive results obtained by goal setting, regardless of whether the feedback is provided by the supervisor or is monitored by the worker himself (48).

Program 5.   Management by Objectives (MBO)

In the past decade, this concept has become prominent in the firmament of good management practice. ⌊Although management by objectives involves the concept of appraisal-and-feedback, the key feature is the definition, in the light of more comprehensive organizational objectives, of performance targets or achievement objectives for each worker's job.⌋ The use of this technique appears to have been spreading, but there have been few experimental evaluations of its effects. Two such studies have appeared in the literature of the past five years, one in industry (40) and another in hospitals (18). Both gave evidence of favorable effects on quality of performance. It is illustrative of the complexities of such programs, however, that grievances increased following installation of the industrial program; and that in the hospitals, after six months, the advantages showed signs of waning.

Program 6.   Goal Setting

This type of program is related both to feedback and to management by objectives.⌋ Goal setting's chief distinguishing feature is the specification of difficult but attainable goals for certain limited--but not unimportant-- aspects of employee performance.⌋ Usually, frequent and specific feedback is given regarding goal attainment.

Recent experiments, mainly in the lumber industry, have consistently shown such programs' positive effects on various aspects of productivity for which goals were set. A limitation is that most of the experiments evaluated

19

Table 4. Program 5: MANAGEMENT BY OBJECTIVES
(numbers refer to abstracts)

Productivity Criterion	Studies Finding Improvement	Studies Not Finding Improvement
Production Quantity	40 (a) blue-collar & sales	
Production Quality	18 (a) nurses 40 (a) blue-collar & sales	
Absenteeism	40 (a) blue-collar & sales	
Grievances		40 (a) blue-collar, sales
Attitudes	18 (a) nurses	

(a)Results mixed, but generally supporting the inference.
(b)Statistical significance not reported or doubtful.
(c)Questionable because of major limitations of experiment.

results over a period of a few months only. One of the most recent studies (57), although again showing that goal setting improved the rate of production, also found indications of deterioration of the job-attitudes of the workers--thus sounding a note of caution regarding possible long-range consequences of setting high goals without making associated improvements that serve to maintain positive motivation. There does not seem to be a difference when goals are assigned vs. participatively set, except possibly that workers from low socioeconomic groups may respond better to the latter (56).

Program 7. Financial Compensation

Pay programs, of course, have a long history as a technique for motivating workers to be productive. The recent studies have focused on specific features bearing on the utility of such programs. Thus, several experiments have confirmed that the linking of compensation to output in some type of incentive plan--a procedure long employed in manufacturing plants--also improves effectiveness of white-collar and service workers (75, 73, 87, 74, 9). Other studies have shown that such systems can also be applied to improving aspects of performance other than output--including absenteeism (97, 71, 88) and tardiness (71); the latter study illustrates a particularly sophisticated and innovative program of financial incentives, one based on behavioral psychology. One study (88) indicates the potential value of having workers participate in designing an incentive pay plan. As a group, these experiments indicate possible ways of further improving, or extending the effectiveness of, programs of financial compensation.

Program 8. Job Design

Over the past decade, the redesign of jobs so as to facilitate worker motivation has been one of the "hot" topics in manpower management. Although

21

Table 5. Program 6: GOAL SETTING
(numbers refer to abstracts)

Productivity Criterion	Studies Finding Improvement	Studies Not Finding Improvement
Production Quantity	54 (b,c) loggers 55 loggers **56 (a) loggers 57 (a) typists 75 (b,c) mental-health workers 79 (b,c) mental-health workers	
Production Quality	48 blue-collar 102 managers	
Production Costs	48 blue-collar	
Turnover		55 loggers
Absenteeism	55 loggers 102 managers	48 blue-collar
Accidents	48 blue-collar	55 loggers
Attitudes	48 blue-collar 102 managers	*57 typists

*Results poorer.
**Improvement in black, less-educated sample but not in white, more-educated one.
(a)Results mixed, but generally supporting the inference.
(b)Statistical significance not reported or doubtful.
(c)Questionable because of major limitations of experiment.

22

Table 6. Program 7: FINANCIAL COMPENSATION
(numbers refer to abstracts)

Productivity Criterion	Studies Finding Improvement	Studies Not Finding Improvement
Production Quantity	9 (c) hospital technicians 73 (b,c) disadvantaged youth 75 (b,c) mental-health workers 103 (a) forestry workers	
Production Quality	**74 (b,c) mental-health workers 87 (a,c) health aides	
Production Costs		39 (b,c) blue-collar *97 (b,c) telephone workers
Absenteeism	71 assemblers 88 (a) custodial workers 97 (b,c) telephone workers	*39 (b,c) blue-collar
Tardiness	71 assemblers	*97 (b,c) telephone workers

*Poorer results.
**Improvement took place only when cash awards were contingent on results.
(a)Results mixed, but generally supporting the inference.
(b)Statistical significance not reported or doubtful.
(c)Questionable because of major limitations of experiment.

job redesign is usually espoused as a way to improve the quality of work-life, it has also been claimed by some adherents to be effective in improving performance--an assertion that has had mixed support in the literature.

Not surprisingly, during the period under review, this topic has been among the liveliest areas of research. Some of the more persuasive experiments listed in Table 7 (e.g., 14, 42, 43, 81, 50, 37) have shown that jobs may be redesigned so as to have favorable effects on one or more aspects of productivity. And by and large, the published research cites more instances of positive effects on various aspects of performance than it does instances of insignificant or adverse effects. Many studies reporting favorable results, however, were case studies in which a number of changes seem to have occurred and which lacked control or comparison groups to make possible an assessment of the causes of the reported results.

There is also the possibility that in general, the cases that are published are those that found positive results (people tend not to publicize their failures). Support for this possibility comes from a recent survey by Hackman; on visiting a number of organizations that had tried to redesign jobs, he discovered that "job enrichment is failing at least as often as it is succeeding."[6]

In short, whether job redesign serves to improve productivity may depend on a number of considerations, including the features of the design; the characteristics of the workers; the nature of the work or technology; and the way the changes are introduced. Not least among these circumstances

---

[6]Hackman, J.R. On the coming demise of job enrichment. Technical Report No. 9, Department of Administrative Sciences, Yale University, 1974, p. 2.

Table 7.   Program 8:   JOB DESIGN
(numbers refer to abstracts)

Productivity Criterion	Studies Finding Improvement	Studies Not Finding Improvement
Production Quantity	14 (c) typists 22 (b,c) telephone workers 25 (c) factory workers 42 (b) typists 44 (b) keypunchers 51 (c) clerks 60 (b,c) inspectors 81 (c) keypunchers & clerks 86 (b,c) factory workers	*7 (a) assemblers 85 (a) tax examiners
Production Quality	16 (b,c) bookkeepers 22 (b,c) telephone workers 25 (c) factory workers 37 (c) air force 42 (b) typists 43 clerks 44 (b) keypunchers 51 (c) clerks 60 (b,c) inspectors 64 (b,c) clerks	7 (a) assemblers 14 (c) typists 85 (a) tax examiners
Production Costs	13 (c) hospital workers 14 (c) typists 25 (c) factory workers 37 air force 44 (b) keypunchers 50 (a) factory workers 51 (c) clerks 64 (b,c) clerks 81 (c) keypunchers, clerks	
Turnover	13 (b,c) hospital workers 22 (b,c) telephone workers 43 (b) clerks 51 (c) clerks	*44 (b) keypunchers

Table 7. Program 8: JOB DESIGN (cont'd.)
(numbers refer to abstracts)

Productivity Criterion	Studies Finding Improvement	Studies Not Finding Improvement
Absenteeism	13 (b,c) hospital workers 22 (b,c) telephone workers 44 (b) keypunchers	50 factory workers
Attitudes	14 (c) typists 42 (b) typists	*7 (a) assemblers 85 tax examiners

*Results poorer.
(a)Results mixed, but generally supporting the inference.
(b)Statistical significance not reported or doubtful.
(c)Questionable because of major limitations of experiment.

are the attitudes and expectations of management; one experiment (50), for example, showed that productivity improvements depended on whether managers were led to expect such gains.

It is interesting that the more traditional approach to job redesign--methods improvement aimed at raising efficiency--was not represented in the experimental literature.

Program 9. Group Design

The experiments under this rubric are also sometimes covered by the term "job enrichment." We have identified here, however, those job-design experiments that featured the redefinition and redistribution of tasks and responsibilities among members of a work group or team--in contrast to changes in individual jobs.

In the present set of studies, the clearest example of this approach is presented in (22). This study cites a number of productivity benefits in the Bell system following what is termed "job nesting" in work groups. Other examples of the approach are furnished in (26, 30, 23). Not all of these efforts were uniformly successful; (23), in particular, illustrates some of the problems.

Program 10. Supervisory Methods

Probably the oldest strategy for changing what goes on in work groups consists of trying to change the way group leaders or supervisors perform their jobs. Among the recent examples of successful techniques for accomplishing this are several of the programs listed and discussed above, including training (38, 28, 102), appraisal and feedback (5, 36), and MBO (102). As an aid to the reader interested in studies on changing supervisory behavior, we cross-list such studies under the present program heading, both in the listing in Table 9, and in the Program Index of Section III.

Table 8.   Program 9:   GROUP DESIGN
(numbers refer to abstracts)

Productivity Criterion	Studies Finding Improvement	Studies Not Finding Improvement
Production Quantity	22 (b) telephone workers 26 (b,c) technicians & blue-collar	
Production Quality	22 (b) telephone workers 26 (b,c) technicians & blue-collar 30 (c) clerks	23 (b) clerks
Turnover	22 (b,c) telephone workers 26 (b,c) technicians & blue-collar	
Absenteeism	22 (b) telephone workers 26 (b,c) technicians & blue-collar	23 (b) clerks
Grievances		30 (c) clerks
Attitudes	30 (c) clerks	22 (b) clerks

(b)Statistical significance not reported or doubtful.
(c)Questionable because of major limitations of experiment.

Table 9. Program 10: SUPERVISORY METHODS
(numbers refer to abstracts)

Productivity Criterion	Studies Finding Improvement	Studies Not Finding Improvement
Production Quantity	5 (b,c) freight-handling workers 8 laundry workers 11 (a,c) factory workers 28 factory workers 38 (b,c) freight-carrier workers 59 (b) retailing workers 78 office workers	76 (a,c) construction & electrical workers
Production Quality	11 (a,c) factory workers 32 factory workers **33 factory workers 36 university workers 38 (b,c) freight-carrier workers 102 hospital workers	
Production Costs	5 (b,c) freight-handling workers 8 laundry workers 13 (b,c) hospital-services workers 59 (b) retailing workers	
Turnover	13 (b,c) hospital-services workers	
Absenteeism	8 laundry workers 13 (b,c) hospital-services workers 102 hospital workers	*76 (a,c) construction & electrical workers
Attitudes	76 (a,c) construction & electrical workers 102 hospital workers	

*Results poorer.
**Improvement under consultative climate, but not under autocratic.
(a)Results mixed, but generally supported the inference.
(b)Statistical significance not reported or doubtful.
(c)Questionable because of major limitations of experiment.

29

Under this rubric, we present the results of several studies aimed at creating increased participation (or "democracy") at the workplace--principally by a change, imposed from above, in policy or procedures. Although there are studies (8, 11, 59) supporting earlier findings that more participative supervision generally gets better results, there is some evidence that this may not always happen (76).

Program 11. Organizational Structure

Like the studies discussed under the program heading immediately above, the studies under the present heading involve imposed policy changes governing working relationships. However, whereas the studies were aimed at the relationships between supervisors and their immediate subordinates, the targets of the present studies are patterns of responsibility and authority among various parts of the organization that are outside, or in addition to, the immediate work-group. In one study (59), for example, structural alteration of management was effected by redesigning the chain of command, creating new roles, and changing existing roles in the management hierarchy. For studies under this rubric, however, these changes are not so extensive as to create a new socio-technical work system, a category covered later.

Since 1971, only five experiments on this difficult but important topic have been reported.

Perhaps the simplest of them is one (88) which gave custodial workers authority to determine the wage-incentive system under which they worked, (hitherto a management privilege); as noted earlier, in the discussion of compensation studies, that shift in authority-structure had positive effects on absenteeism, which was the target outcome.

30

Table 10.   Program 11: ORGANIZATIONAL STRUCTURE
(numbers refer to abstracts)

Productivity Criterion	Studies Finding Improvement	Studies Not Finding Improvement
Production Quantity	45 (c) telephone workers 58 (c) auto-assembly workers 59 (b) retailing workers 89 (b,c) mental-health-center workers	
Production Quality	58 (c) auto-assembly workers	
Production Costs	58 (c) auto-assembly workers 59 (b) retailing workers	
Absenteeism	∠88 (a) custodial workers	
Grievances	58 (c) auto-assembly workers	

(a)Results mixed, but generally supporting the inference.
(b)Statistical significance not reported or doubtful.
(c)Questionable because of major limitations of experiment.

At the other extreme is a case (89) in which a health-service system was made more productive by reorganization featuring both the integration of certain previously separate responsibilities, and the decentralization of operational responsibility and authority among five separate units.

Two other experiments further serve to illustrate the productivity value of integrating certain previously specialized functions. One (58) involved the reconstitution of certain manufacturing groups; the other (45) involved the formation of cross-functional coordinating task forces in a white-collar operation.

The foregoing experiments support the long-held tenet of the importance of proper organizational structure, but unfortunately, experimental evaluations of alternative forms remain rare.

Program 12. Physical Working-Conditions

In the past, considerable attention has been given to the productivity consequences of various physical working conditions, such as illumination, noise, layout, etc. Indeed, even the classic Hawthorne studies started in that vein. Oddly enough, we located no reports published between 1971 and 1975 of field experiments on such programs, and so we present no table corresponding to that rubric.

Program 13. Work Schedule

One topic that has survived from the classic domain of physical conditions of work has to do with time spent at work. In its current form, this topic has focused mainly on the effects of shifting to the so-called 4/40 plan, i.e., scheduling work shifts to consist of four ten-hour workdays per week. In recent years, more than one hundred companies have moved to this pattern;[7] another survey[8] shows that twenty-two of twenty-seven firms where this pattern was followed had good experiences with it.

Several experiments in our review (95, 63, 41) reported favorable effects on quantity, quality, and/or costs of production. Favorable effects were not, however, universal (10, 53). Effects on turnover (63, 95) and on absenteeism (41, 95, 68) were also equivocal. One of the experiments (68) found also that employees developed negative attitudes toward the plan; a recent survey[9] indicates differences in the attitudes of different segments of the work force (e.g., more women opposed the plan than did men).

Another experimental work-schedule receiving recent attention has been called "flexi-time." Under flexi-time, workers are expected to put in a standard number of hours per day or week; but except for a fixed core-period in the middle of the day, they are free to arrive or leave as they please (or as negotiated with the supervisor). This type of plan has been fairly widely adopted in Europe, but not in the United States.[10] An experimental study of the plan in one American company (29) indicated that flexi-time had positive effects on production costs and on absenteeism, but did not affect turnover.

Finally, experiments are beginning to appear in which work-time is used as an incentive to good performance. In one experiment (9), hospital lab-technicians were given time-off for keeping up with service requests; as a

---

[7]Gurman, R. and Tarnowieski, R. The four day week. New York: American Management Associations, 1972.

[8]Poor, R. Reporting a revolution in work and leisure: 27 4-day firms. In R. Poor (ed.), 4 days, 40 hours. Cambridge, Mass.: Burck & Poor, 1970.

[9]Dickinson, T.L. and Wijting, J.P. An analysis of workers' attitudes toward the 4-day, 40-hour workweek. Psychological Reports, 1975, 37, 383-390.

[10]Glickman, A.S. and Brown, Z.H. Changing schedules of work: Patterns and implications. Washington: Upjohn Institute, 1974.

Table 11. Program 13: WORK SCHEDULE
(numbers refer to abstracts)

Productivity Criterion	Studies Finding Improvement	Studies Not Finding Improvement
Production Quantity	9 (c) hospital-lab workers 31 (b,c) hospital workers 63 (b,c) insurance workers 95 (b,c) factory workers	10 (c) factory workers 53 (b,c) office workers
Production Quality	63 (b,c) insurance workers 41 (a) factory workers	
Production Costs	29 Research & Development units 95 (b,c) factory workers	*97 (b,c) telephone workers
Turnover	63 (b,c) insurance workers	29 Research & Development units 95 (b,c) factory workers
Absenteeism	29 Research & Development units 31 (b,c) hospital workers 68 (c) pharmaceuticals workers 97 (a,b,c) telephone workers	41 factory workers *95 (b,c) factory workers
Tardiness	95 (b,c) factory workers	*97 (b,c) telephone workers
Attitudes	29 Research & Development units 41 factory workers	*68 (c) pharmaceuticals workers

*Results poorer.
(a)Results mixed, but generally supporting the inference.
(b)Statistical significance not reported or doubtful.
(c)Questionable because of major limitations of experiment.

result, there was an improvement in their record of completing work. In a similar vein (97), telephone-company workers were awarded time-off (or the cash equivalent) for compiling specified numbers of consecutive-days-without-absence, with the result that attendance improved somewhat (although not enough to overcome the program's cost).

These last two studies suggest that at least to some extent with some workers, time may be interchangeable with money as an incentive-to-performance. However, the overall picture of the productivity consequences of revised work-schedules remains unclear.

Program 14. Socio-Technical System

Here we turn to programs involving changes of sufficient magnitude in a large number of salient variables as to constitute a revised socio-technical system of work. Twelve such experiments qualified for our review. Unfortunately, even these typically took the form of single case studies, lacking comparison or control groups that would help pin down whether the new system was truly the cause of the observed results, or whether there were other possible explanations (such as changes in the economy, technological improvements, organizational "learning" from experience, etc.). On the other hand, each of these experiments furnished sufficient factual data to qualify it as more than someone's impressionistic testimonial. Thus, while no one of these experiments could by itself constitute firm proof, clear and convergent results from several would have to be regarded as strongly suggestive (even if not completely persuasive).

As shown in Table 12, only one of the studies had uniformly negative results. The other eleven reported improvement in an average of three productivity measures each. The specific features of the experiments that succeeded

35

Table 12. Program 14: SOCIO-TECHNICAL SYSTEM
(numbers refer to abstracts)

Productivity Criterion	Studies Finding Improvement	Studies Not Finding Improvement
Production Quantity	11 (a,c) manufacturing workers 15 (c) auto-manufacturing workers 24 (c) manufacturing workers 34 (c) welfare-administration workers 47 (b,c) food-processing workers 77 (c) manufacturing workers 93 (c) welfare-administration workers 98 (c) glass-manufacturing workers	49 (a,c) auto-manufacturing workers 61 (c) manufacturing workers
Production Quality	11 (a,c) manufacturing workers 15 (c) auto-manufacturing workers 34 (c) welfare-administration workers 49 (a,c) auto-manufacturing workers 93 (c) welfare-administration workers 99 (c) food-manufacturing workers 101 (c) custodial workers	
Production Costs	15 (c) auto-manufacturing workers 24 (c) manufacturing workers 34 (c) welfare-administration workers 47 (b,c) food-processing workers 49 (a,c) auto-manufacturing workers 93 (c) welfare-administration workers 99 (c) food-manufacturing workers 101 (c) custodial workers	*61 (c) manufacturing workers
Turnover	47 (b,c) food-processing workers 94 (b,c) office workers 101 (c) custodial workers	35 (a,c) lumber workers 61 (c) manufacturing workers
Absenteeism	24 (c) manufacturing workers 35 (a,c) lumber workers 47 (b,c) food-processing workers 93 (c) welfare-administration workers	61 (c) manufacturing workers
Tardiness	24 (c) manufacturing workers 93 (c) welfare-administration workers	

Table 12.   Program 14:   SOCIO-TECHNICAL SYSTEM (cont'd.)
(numbers refer to abstracts)

Productivity Criterion	Studies Finding Improvement	Studies Not Finding Improvement
Grievances	15 (c) auto-manufacturing workers	
Attitudes	15 (c) auto-manufacturing workers 35 (c) lumber workers 99 (b,c) food-manufacturing workers	

*Results poorer.
(a)Results mixed, but generally supporting the inference.
(b)Statistical significance not reported or doubtful.
(c)Questionable because of major limitations of experiment.

vary from program to program, but certain elements keep recurring: redesign of jobs and of teams; wider sharing of responsibility, influence, and authority; compilation and distribution of information about goals, problems, and results; improvements in operations; selection of competent personnel; and training and development of workers at various levels. In at least one instance (24), there were financial benefits directly linked to improved performance, and in another (34, 93) there was a tightening-up of account-ability and of discipline; but these were not regular themes.

In short, extensive and integrated combinations of various of the pre-viously discussed programs appear to generate socio-technical systems which, in nearly all cases, are reported to have had markedly favorable effects on various aspects of productivity. The typical absence of comparison groups raises questions of causality. Still, the sources indicate the promise of such an approach.

Summary and Conclusions

The literature of the past five years furnished factual reports of 103 experiments aimed at improving worker productivity in the United States. Although manufacturing industries continue to be the most active in conducting such studies, the level of activity in other sectors has grown beyond a trickle. It is especially interesting that 20 of the 103 reports came from non-profit organizations such as hospitals or clinics, while 9 other reports dealt with public agencies--suggesting distinct concern for the improvement of productivity in the service sector.

Eighty-five of the experiments reported favorable effects on one or more aspects of productivity. This is an encouraging picture, for it indicates that the improvement of worker performance--a result that should benefit all segments of society--is attainable through strategies already within our grasp.

But a note of caution must be sounded. The limitations of many of the experiments raise questions about the validity or generalizability of their findings. Furthermore, not all were successful, and one wonders how many other failures never were written up for publication.

This leads to the question of what kinds of programs gave the greatest evidence of success. For convenience, we classified the programs into fourteen categories, two of which--promotional systems and physical working conditions--turned out to be represented little or not at all in the literature under review. Of the others, an old standby--training--was the most frequently used, followed closely by the newer strategy of redesigning jobs so as to render them more motivating to workers.

The earlier pages of this chapter summarized the results obtained via these various programs. By way of even further summarization, we note the

39

following trends or developments as tentative conclusions:

--Applications of behavioral analysis are becoming more popular, with substantial evidence of their value. The chief elements in this approach include identifying for the worker what effective behavior is; providing him with occasions to enact it; furnishing prompt and frequent feedback regarding results; and giving material or symbolic rewards contingent on effective performance. Specific programs incorporating these elements include training techniques such as behavior modification, modeling, and motive acquisition, as well as certain appraisal-and-compensation plans.

--Another behavioral principle whose application appears to be producing useful results is the setting of clear and difficult-but-attainable goals for performance. This principle is involved in management by objectives, as well as in the simpler type of program called goal setting. Like behavioral analysis, goal setting typically involves prompt and frequent feedback.

--The redesign of jobs, either of individuals or of work teams, often has beneficial effects, but fails in a significant proportion of instances. Apparently, job redesign is likely to fail unless there is a commitment, on the part of all concerned, to make it work; unless the redesign is more than superficial; and unless the program is congruent with other elements in the system--kinds of workers, technology, labor relations, etc.

--Financial compensation continues to be a major influence on worker productivity, particularly when creative ways are devised to have pay be contingent upon performance.

--The wider sharing of responsibility and control, sometimes called participative management, is more than a philosophy--it usually is found to have positive results, as well.

--Organizational structures that integrate functions and decentralize authority show promise.

--It is advisable that any plan to improve and maintain productivity be approached in terms of the total socio-technical work system itself--that is, the interrelated set of psychological, social, technological, economic, and cultural factors which must be integrated and harmonized if the system is to be effective over the long haul. Viewed in that way, specific productivity-programs which may work in some situations may fail in others. Therefore, achieving major improvements in productivity may often require revising the system, making certain that each new step is consistent with its predecessors and with the whole. Eventually, such an approach is likely to entail application of many, if not all, of the fourteen kinds of programs discussed earlier. The overall results of eleven experiments, each of which involved change in a number of program elements, support the utility of this strategy for the improvement of worker productivity.

SECTION II

ABSTRACTS OF PRODUCTIVITY EXPERIMENTS

CHAPTER 3

DESCRIPTION OF ABSTRACTS

This Section presents short abstracts of the 103 experiments that met the criteria stated in Chapter 1. The order of presentation is alphabetical by surname of (first) author. In the upper right-hand corner of each abstract appears the abstract number (ranging from 1 to 103) by which the report is also identified elsewhere in this document. In the upper left-hand corner are coded the types of workers and of organizations involved (we employ the coding systems of the Dictionary of Occupational Titles (DOT) and the Standard Industrial Code (SIC), explained further in the respective indexes contained in Section IV). Also in the upper left-hand corner are program code-numbers identifying the kind of program or innovation tried, and criterion code-numbers identifying the kind of outcome in terms of which the effects were studied (these two sets of codes, introduced in Chapter 2, are further explained under 5 and 8, below).

The body of each abstract comprises eleven parts or paragraphs, as follows:

1. <u>Bibliographical reference</u>: author(s), title, and journal (if an article) or publisher (if a book or monograph).

2. <u>Conclusions</u>: a brief statement of the principal implications of the findings. Being brief, this statement does not refer to all of the limitations and equivocations to which virtually all experimental results are subject. For each experiment, chief limitations are summarized in paragraph 11 of the abstract, as explained under 11, below. When, however, we believe that the experiment's limitations are sufficiently marked as to render the conclusion rather tentative or doubtful, an asterisk at the end

of the conclusion directs the reader's special attention to paragraph 11. These succinct conclusions should, then, be interpreted as saying something like, "All in all, the results of this experiment indicate that the following is probably true...."--or (when an asterisk is used), "...tentatively suggest that the following may be true...." In every case, the conclusion should be understood to be subject to at least the caveats noted in paragraph 11 of each abstract. One caveat so universal that it goes without saying is the fact that each conclusion is situation-bound: it emerges from an experiment done in a particular industry, with a particular work force, etc. and may not, therefore, be generalizable to a different situation. On the other hand, it does suggest what may be true or useful in that new situation.

3. Organization: a statement of the name (if given) or of the type of organization in which the study was conducted. (That information served as the basis on which the company was assigned the SIC number coded in the upper left-hand corner.)

4. Workers: a statement of the kinds or occupations of workers studied. (To the extent made possible by the specificity, that information served as the basis for assigning the DOT codes shown in the upper left-hand corner.)

5. Program: a brief description of the new procedure or treatment tried. These were then classified into one or more of fourteen program types (code number(s) are given in the upper left-hand corner). The fourteen programs, together with their code numbers, are as follows:

Program 1. Selection and placement: changes in how the organization is staffed (including any of the activities associated with recruitment, selection, and placement).

Program 2. Job development and promotion: new or different systems of providing career or promotional opportunities for workers.

46

Program 3. Training and instruction: programmed learning experiences designed to assist groups of workers in acquiring new or additional information, attitudes, or skills.

Program 4. Appraisal and feedback: techniques of furnishing individuals with information about their job performance, typically with the intent of helping them to learn how to do their jobs better.

Program 5. Management by objectives: identification of the outcomes or results that individuals are expected to achieve in their jobs, typically by a supervisor in consultation with the incumbent, and often coupled with periodic feedback.

Program 6. Goal setting: the specification of difficult but attainable goals for certain limited (but not unimportant) aspects of performance of individuals or teams of employees; often coupled with feedback on degree of goal attainment.

Program 7. Financial compensation: direct monetary inducements for working, typically in the form of wages, salaries, and/or bonuses or commissions.

Program 8. Job design: the specification of tasks, duties, and responsibilities that workers are expected to perform in their jobs. Job enrichment aims at making jobs more complex or challenging. Job enlargement aims at increasing their variety or diversity. Job-methods improvement is intended to facilitate the execution of work.

Program 9. Group design: the distribution of responsibility, authority, and/or activities among members of a work group or team, exclusive of supervisory relationships.

Program 10. Supervisory methods: that aspect of work group design that pertains to relationships between the group supervisor or leader and the other members, focusing on the behavior or style of the supervisor. Often, changes in supervisory methods are induced by other programs, such as training or feedback; in that case, the study is categorized under both headings. Studies classified solely under the rubric "supervisory methods" typically change those methods by means of policies or prescriptions imposed from above.

Program 11. Organizational structure: refers to experiments in which patterns of responsibility, authority, and/or functions have been redistributed among various segments of the organization outside of, or in addition to, the face-to-face work groups. The modifications are typically introduced in one or two dimensions of structure--such as authority ("participation")--and so are too limited to be regarded as a redesigned socio-technical system as in 14, below.

Program 12. Physical working conditions: alterations of the physical environment or facilities.

Program 13. Work schedule: changes in the number and/or distribution of hours worked per day or per week.

Program 14. Socio-technical system: pervasive alterations in a number of salient aspects of the human resources, work methods, social relations, and organizational structure—which, in aggregate, constitute a new system. The dimensions of change ordinarily include a number of the thirteen specific programs listed above.

6. Method: refers to how the program was devised and installed, e.g., by management, by a labor-management committee, etc.

7. Design: in addition to knowing the content (program) of the experiment and the method by which the change was made, it is relevant to know how the experiment was designed—that is, when the measurements were taken, whether they were made on control as well as on experimental groups, etc. Such information is briefly reported in this paragraph.

8. Productivity results: here we summarize the changes in the criteria or outcome variables pertaining to productivity; this, of course, is the payoff.

9. Other results: in addition to reporting productivity results, some experiments reported other results which may be of interest—job attitudes, gross margin, etc. When available, these results are noted in this paragraph.

10. Intervening factors: in interpreting why certain results were or were not obtained, it is useful to know whether changes occurred in certain intervening or mediating variables which may link the experimental changes or program to the criterion variables or outcomes. Examples of such intervening variables might be reports of greater interest on the part of workers, or supervisors' estimates that it was harder to meet deadlines. Such information is not often provided, but when provided, it is furnished under this heading.

11. Limitations: it is a truism that no perfect experiment has ever been conducted; the experiments under review have not given us cause to re-

vise that statement. In this section are summarized the principal methodo-logical weaknesses or deficiences that we note in each experiment, so that the reader may be alerted to limitations to the validity or applicability of the results. The presence of deficiencies should not be taken to mean that the experiment was worthless; such studies have been excluded from our report. Nor should the noting of deficiencies necessarily be interpreted as a criticism of the authors. It is true that there were all too many instances in which the research could have been improved by the application of known techniques --thus pointing to the need for having trained researchers in-volved in the conduct of such experiments. But often there are insuperable problems in conducting field experiments. Indeed, all these efforts are to be applauded even if not completely successful--would that more organizations would undertake systematic productivity experiments worthy of publication. What the noting of limitations does mean is that the conclusion should be taken with a grain of salt--or with several grains, if the limitations were sufficiently grave (as with the abstracts marked with footnote c in the tables of Chapter 2). In the present paragraph, we employ a standard system of noting deficiencies, as follows:

A. Absence of control group(s): means that there was no equivalent group of workers on whom the experiment was not tried or who were exposed to a different treatment. As a consequence, one cannot be sure that the ob-served results were due to the experimental changes, rather than to other causes. This is a serious threat to the credibility of the findings, which should be given weight only when supported by other studies.

B. Non-equivalence of comparison group(s): designates experiments which employed groups which were not given the experimental treatment, but which were not truly control groups because they were not quite equivalent to

49

the experimental group in their makeup. Having such groups for comparison is better than having none at all, but it still is subject to erroneous inferences--because the differences in results may be due to the differences in makeup rather than to differences in treatment.

C. Peculiarities of measurement: refers to characteristics of the techniques used for measuring the results. These peculiarities of measurement were of two general types: fallible measures which seem prone to yield erroneous information, or highly specialized or unusual measures which may not have much meaning for the other organizations. Such peculiarities are specified in the abstract.

D. Peculiarities of program: refers to features of the innovation which either may not be readily adaptable elsewhere or which entail elements not ordinarily or necessarily associated with that type of program, as when training is coupled with goal setting. Such peculiarities are specified.

E. Peculiarities of the sample: refers to special characteristics of the workers or of the work setting that may account for the results obtained, but that may limit their generalizability elsewhere. To some extent, virtually all experiments are prone to this limitation, which means that due caution should be observed in exporting their results. We therefore note these peculiarities only if they are extreme or unusual to suggest that in many other situations, the results may not be replicable.

F. Statistical inadequacies: refers to instances when the result of an experiment may be erroneous on statistical grounds, i.e., the effect may be more apparent than real. The main culprit here was the failure to do statistical tests of significance when the data base was sufficiently small as to suggest the distinct possibility of a chance result.

The 103 abstracts, containing the above information in summary form, follow.

50

DOT: 502   #1
SIC: D-33
Program: 4
Criterion: 1,2,3,15

1. Reference: Adam, E.E., Jr.   Behavior modification in quality control.
   Academy of Management Journal, 1975, 18, 662-679.

2. Conclusions: The use of verbal reinforcement (feedback) during weekly
   meetings of foremen and operators can lead to increased quantity of
   performance, but effects on quality of performance and on employee
   satisfaction were not demonstrated.*

3. Organization: Midwestern diecasting manufacturing facility, with
   diecasting, production and packing operations.

4. Workers: Three shifts of diecasting department, with a range of eight
   to 14 employees in any one shift, and with overall numbers ranging from
   28 to 39.

5. Program: Verbal reinforcement by foremen during weekly meetings in
   which operators received feedback regarding quantity and quality data;
   comparisons were made between individual operator, shift and department; quality was emphasized and information discussions were held.

6. Method: Installed by management and consultants.

7. Design: For 45 weeks, weekly measures of production were obtained,
   with the program being introduced at week nine; non-equivalent control
   group used for assessing attitudinal data.

8. Productivity Results: Comparison of the seven weeks prior to and the
   seven weeks following intervention showed no significant differences in
   quality of production; significant improvement was found in quantity of
   production; projected overall annual savings of $77,000.

9. Other Results: Use of the Job Descriptive Index showed negligible
   attitude differences between experimental and control groups and within the experimental group over time.

10. Intervening Effects: No significant difference was found in employees'
    attitude toward production quantity over time or between groups; in
    general, insignificant results for attitude toward quality.

*11. Limitations: A. Absence of control group in analysis of production
                       changes.
                    B. Non-equivalence of comparison groups for attitude data.

1. Reference: Alander, R., & Campbell, T. An evaluative study of an alcohol and drug recovery program: A case study of the Oldsmobile experience. Human Resource Management, 1975, 14(1), 14-18.

2. Conclusions: An alcoholism rehabilitation program appears to have been
   useful in reducing lost wages, leaves of absence, grievances, and disciplinary actions, but not in reducing accident rate.

3. Organization: Oldsmobile Division of General Motors Corporation in
   Lansing, Michigan.

4. Workers: 117 hourly workers who after an interview volunteered to be in
   the experimental rehabilitation program. The non-equivalent comparison
   group consisted of 24 workers who were known to management as alcohol or
   drug users but who did not volunteer.

5. Program: Oldsmobile Employee Alcoholism Recovery Program: supervisors
   were trained to recognize performance problems related to alcohol/drugs.
   Problem employees were referred by their supervisor to the Personnel
   Section, where they had a talk with the plant physician. Contact was
   made with outside agencies; this was followed by support by the company
   for employee and family. When employee was released from agency, or if
   employee was an outpatient, employee was examined by plant physician.

6. Method: Installed by management and union (United Auto Workers).

7. Design: Before-and-after measurements, using a non-equivalent control
   group.

8. Productivity Results: After one year of the program, wages lost were
   reduced by about $40,000 in the experimental group and were increased
   by over $7,000 in the comparison group. Leaves of absence decreased
   24% in the experimental group and increased 60% in the comparison.
   Grievances decreased 100% in the experimental group and 17% in the
   comparison. Disciplinary actions decreased 70% in the experimental
   group and increased 190% in the comparison. Accidents decreased 85% in
   the experimental group and 80% in the comparison. Program costs
   totaled approximately $57,000 for the year.

9. Other Results: None reported.

10. Intervening Effects: None reported.

11. Limitations: B. Non-equivalence of comparison groups.
                   F. No tests of significance.

1. Reference: Alpert, J.L. Teacher behavior and pupil performance: Reconsideration of the mediation of Pygmalion effects. <u>Journal of Educational Research</u>, 1975, <u>69</u>(2), 53-57.

2. Conclusions: Brief instruction in effective behavior may change the behavior of the trainees, but not necessarily have the expected consequences; this suggests the importance of ascertaining the relevance of the training content.

3. Organization: 13 Catholic schools in New York City.

4. Workers: Experimental group: eight second-grade teachers; comparison group: nine second-grade teachers.

5. Program: Training to increase effective behavior in the teaching of reading; teachers in the experimental group were instructed to follow a list of such behaviors, including giving poorer readers more time daily, more materials, more verbal behaviors, etc.

6. Method: Installed by management and consultants.

7. Design: Before-and-after measures, using control group.

8. Productivity Results: Training of teachers had no effect on vocabulary or comprehension performance of pupils.

9. Other Results: None reported.

10. Intervening Effects: Observation and teacher logs showed that following introduction of program, teachers in experimental group generally used more good non-verbal behaviors.

11. Limitations: B. Equivalence of comparison groups questionable.
    D. Short-term program, only three visits and two phone calls.

1. Reference: Aronoff, J., & Litwin, G.H. Achievement motivation training and executive advancement. _Journal of Applied Behavioral Science_,
   1971, _7_, 215-229.

2. Conclusions: Executives' rate of advancement can be expedited by
   training in achievement motivation.*

3. Organization: A major corporation, unspecified.

4. Workers: Middle-level excutives, ranging in age from 32 to 59. All
   were college graduates; some had done some graduate work.

5. Program: A training course designed to increase the achievement motivation of executives. The course was based on McClelland's theoretical
   principles of motive acquisition. The outline of the program was to
   create a belief in the possibility and desirability of developing increased achievement motivation--helping participants to conceptualize
   clearly what achievement motivation is--and to encourage the participants to set concrete goals. Involved the use of practice exercises.

6. Method: Installed by management.

7. Design: Two years after completion of training, comparison of job
   level and salary attained by participants with matched control group.

8. Productivity Results: Five of the 11 managers in the experimental
   group had a higher rate of advancement (level and salary) than did
   their controls.

9. Other Results: None reported.

10. Intervening Effects: None reported.

*11. Limitations: C. Advancement decisions may have been affected by
                      management's knowledge of whether or not training had
                      been received.
                   E. Small and possibly unrepresentative sample.

DOT: unspecified   #5
SIC: E-451
Program: 4,10
Criterion: 3

1. Reference: At Emery Air Freight: Positive reinforcement boosts performance.   Organizational Dynamics, 1973, 1(3), 41-50.

2. Conclusions: Positive verbal reinforcement of specific production-
   related behaviors may result in productivity improvements and in cost
   savings.*

3. Organization: Emery Air Freight.

4. Workers: In sales and sales training; operations; and containerized
   shipments.

5. Program: Performance audit followed by behavior modification through
   positive reinforcement (praise and recognition by managers) of specific
   work behaviors.   Managers were given two programmed-instruction work-
   books enumerating kinds of reinforcement to be used.

6. Method: Installed by management.

7. Design: Before-and-after measures of experimental groups only.

8. Productivity Results: In sales, there was a more rapid rate of gain;
   in operations, standards of improved customer-service were met 90-95%
   of the time, compared with previous 30-40%, and performance averaged
   90-95% in the majority of customer-service offices after four years;
   in containerized shipping operations, container use increased from
   45% to 95%.   Estimated savings over three years was $3 million.

9. Other Results: None reported.

10. Intervening Effects: None reported.

*11. Limitations: A. Absence of control group.
                    C. Evaluative data not detailed.
                    F. No tests of significance.

V 1. Reference: Beatty, R.W. A two-year study of hard-core-unemployed
   clerical workers: Effects of scholastic achievement, clerical skill,
   and self-esteem on job success. Personnel Psychology, 1975, 28, 165-
   174.

2. Conclusions: The training of hard-core-unemployed clerical workers may
   result in improved ability and in long-term job success (evaluations
   and earnings).*

3. Organization: Medium-sized insurance company.

4. Workers: Experimental group composed of females with background of
   hard-core unemployment; began with 41 and ended two years later with
   23; comparison group consisted of 40 regular hires; both groups were in
   clerical positions.

5. Program: 18-week, 300-hour basic-education training, plus on-the-job
   training.

6. Method: Installed by management.

7. Design: For both groups, supervisory performance-ratings were determined after six months and again after two years on job; and weekly
   earnings, after two years.

8. Productivity Results: After six months, experimental group had significantly lower evaluations than comparison group; however, after two
   years, experimental group was significantly higher on evaluations and
   had significantly higher earnings than comparison group.

9. Other Results: None reported.

10. Intervening Effects: Significant improvement for experimental group in
    tests of scholastic achievement and of clerical skill, not in measure
    of self-esteem. Scholastic achievement predictive of two-year weekly
    earnings but not of job performance. Clerical skill predictive of
    evaluations but not of earnings.

*11. Limitations: B. Non-equivalence of comparison groups.
               C. Supervisory ratings and earnings.

DOT: 709
SIC: I-833
Program: 8
Criterion: 1,2,15

1. Reference: Bishop, R.C., & Hill, J.W. Effects of job enlargement and job change in contiguous but nonmanipulated jobs as a function of workers' status. Journal of Applied Psychology, 1971, 55, 175-181.

2. Conclusions: Job enlargement may have adverse effects on quantity and quality of productivity. Job satisfaction and status of adjacent workers whose jobs remain unchanged may decline, although their productivity may not suffer.*

3. Organization: Employment Training Center at Southern Illinois University--a sheltered workshop for the rehabilitation of mentally and physically handicapped people.

4. Workers: 48 handicapped workers on light bench-work.

5. Program: Compared effects of job enlargement with effects of a simple job change on both manipulated and nonmanipulated jobs; workers in the latter jobs were aware of the changes in others' jobs.

6. Method: Installed by management.

7. Design: Random assignment of the 48 workers to eight work groups. Measures of job satisfaction, job performance (quantity and quality), and tension were taken.

8. Productivity Results: Quantity and quality of production were significantly lower for the enlarged jobs; job changes without enlargement reduced quality but not quantity.

9. Other Results: Job satisfaction declined in the group whose jobs remained the same, but not in the other groups.

10. Intervening Effects: The correlation between number of errors and task complexity was significant, suggesting a partial explanation of the decrement in quality of performance for those doing the enlarged task. Those workers whose jobs were changed reported less tension; those whose jobs remained the same reported more tension, paralleling their lowered job satisfaction. The latter group also lost some social status.

*11. Limitations: D. Short duration of program.
              E. Sheltered workshop for rehabilitation.
              F. Small sample.

1. Reference: Bragg, J.E. & Andrews, I.R. Participative decision making:
   An experimental study in a hospital. Journal of Applied Behavioral
   Science, 1973, 9, 727-735.

2. Conclusions: After introduction of participative decision making in a
   small department, absenteeism decreased and productivity increased. The
   result was a reduction in costs.

3. Organization: Hospital laundry.

4. Workers: 32 unionized laundry workers. Laundries in two other hospitals served as comparison groups.

5. Program: Introduction of participative decision-making program in place
   of the traditional authority system. Some decision-making power was
   shifted from the laundry foreman to a committee of laundry employees.

6. Method: Installed by management, with union approval.

7. Design: Attitudinal measures taken every two months during 18-month
   experimental period. Records of absenteeism and of productivity of all
   participants were compared prior to and during the experiment.

8. Productivity Results: In the experimental group, absenteeism (compared
   to the overall hospital rate) increased initially, but then significantly decreased; the productivity rate improved gradually. Comparison
   groups showed a slight decrease during the period studied.

9. Other Results: Cost savings per employee estimated at $1,000 per year
   were attributed to the program.

10. Intervening Effects: After initial uncertainty, employees reported pos-
    itive attitudes toward the program.

11. Limitations: B. Non-equivalence of comparison groups.

1. Reference: Burroughs, W.A., & Richardson, P. Behavior modification in a clinical laboratory. Hospital Administration, 1975, 20(3), 54-59.

2. Conclusions: When time off was used as a reinforcer, performance of laboratory technicians seems to have improved. The effects wore off when the reinforcement was discontinued.*

3. Organization: 865-bed hospital.

4. Workers: 11 technicians, including 10 full-time staff members (nine female, one male) and one full-time supervisor (female). Ages ranged from 19 to 33 years. Primary function was collecting blood samples for lab testing.

5. Program: Behavior modification: reinforcement by giving staff time off for doing a good job. Performance was determined by the number of unfilled requests for blood samples at the end of each shift. No unfilled requests for two consecutive days was reinforced by giving 15 minutes off; for four consecutive days by giving 45 minutes off; and for six consecutive days by giving 75 minutes off.

6. Method: Installed by management.

7. Design: Time-series measures before, during and after reinforcement period (three-week duration).

8. Productivity Results: Significantly fewer unfilled requests occurred during, as compared with before, the program. Significantly fewer unfilled requests occurred during, as compared with after, the contingency period, indicating return to the prior level of performance.

9. Other Results: None reported.

10. Intervening Effects: None reported.

*11. Limitations: A. Absence of control group.
                 E. Small and possibly unrepresentative sample.

DOT: 786
SIC: D-23
Program: 13
Criterion: 1

1. Reference: Calvasina, E.J., & Boxx, W.R. Efficiency of workers on the four-day workweek. Academy of Management Journal, 1975, 18, 604-609.

2. Conclusions: Change to a four-day workweek did not influence the productivity of production workers.*

3. Organization: Two factories of a firm that manufactured wearing apparel.

4. Workers: Experienced female production workers engaged in the sewing of garments; 64 at Factory 1 and 103 at Factory 2.

5. Program: Change from a five-day, 40-hour workweek to a four-day, 38-hour workweek.

6. Method: Installed by management.

7. Design: Production data collected for experimental groups only, for a one-year period before and for a one-year period after the new work schedule.

8. Productivity Results: For both factories, there was no significant difference in quantity of production in the two periods.

9. Other Results: None reported.

10. Intervening Effects: None reported.

*11. Limitations: A. Absence of control group.

DOT: unspecified   #11
SIC: D-36
Program: 10,14
Criterion: 1,2

1. Reference: Chaney, F., & Teel, K. Participative management--a practical experience. Personnel, 1972, 49, 8-19.

2. Conclusions: Quantity and quality of production were significantly improved by comprehensive changes in the management system, principally featuring a more participative approach on the part of first-level supervisors.

3. Organization: Autonetics, a division of North American Rockwell.

4. Workers: Various work groups participating in the program. No other information provided.

5. Program: Participative management. Key elements were (a) Management orientation. (b) Supervisory seminars. (c) Supervisor group meetings emphasizing performance measurement, problem solving and goal setting. (d) Coaching of supervisors by staff psychologists. (e) Management follow-up.

6. Method: Installed at first level of supervision. Upper management was to withhold interference of judgment and to observe supervisors' efforts.

7. Design: Study describes in detail the steps listed in the program. Performance data gathered over four years are presented.

8. Productivity Results: 27 groups showed statistically significant performance gains; 12 showed no significant change, and one showed a significant decrease. In groups that increased significantly, gains averaged 20-30% increase in production and 30-50% decline in errors.

9. Other Results: Groups showing a significant performance gain also expressed more positive attitudes toward the company and toward being involved in the program.

10. Intervening Effects: None reported.

11. Limitations: A. Absence of control group.

1. Reference: Cook, D.W., Kunce, J.T., & Sleater, S.M. Vicarious behavior induction and training psychiatric aides. _Journal of Community Psychology_, 1974, 2, 293-297.

2. Conclusions: Training inexperienced workers through modeling of effective behavior shown on videotape showed a better result than training by means of discussion alone.*

3. Organization: Midwestern state hospital.

4. Workers: 33 psychiatric-aide trainees; nearly all with high school education; age range, 18 to mid-forties.

5. Program: Trainees were assigned to one of three groups, all of which were given nine written lessons describing topics relevant to effective interpersonal skills. (a) Discussion group: discussed nine lessons, one at each of nine 30-minute sessions. (b) Didactic-and-discussion group: during each session, discussed lesson and viewed five-minute videotaped lecture. (c) Vicarious-induction group: during each session, viewed five-minute videotape that presented models demonstrating behavior described in lessons.

6. Method: Installed by management and consultants.

7. Design: Random assignment of 11 aides to each of three training groups, with competency measures taken during subsequent six weeks of on-the-job performance as ward aides.

8. Productivity Results: Mean performance-rating of vicarious-induction (modeling) group was significantly higher only than that of the discussion-alone group; didactic-and-discussion group was intermediate.

9. Other Results: None reported.

10. Intervening Effects: Instructors preferred modeling; no clearcut differences in students' attitudes.

*11. Limitations: B. Non-equivalence of comparison groups.
                   C. Limitations of rating criteria.
                   E. Inexperienced trainees; work featured interpersonal skills.

DOT: 31,187
SIC: I-806
Program: 3,8,10
Criterion: 3,5,6

1. Reference: Copenhaver, J.R. Training, job enrichment reduce costs. Hospitals, 1973, 47(3), 118, 122, 126.

2. Conclusions: Providing supervisors with management training and implementing job changes may reduce costs, absenteeism and turnover.*

3. Organization: George Washington University Hospital, Washington, D.C.

4. Workers: 12 supervisors; workers in three sections of food services department (supply, preparation and patient service; cafeteria; dieticians).

5. Program: Phase 1 (supervisory training): supervisors and food administrators met in weekly two-hour sessions during one year; training director taught management theory, which trainees applied to actual cases. Phase 2 (job enrichment): time studies were carried out for workers in three sections, with appropriate changes in job definitions and duties and with new career ladders for promotion.

6. Method: Installed by University training director and by food service/hospital administration.

7. Design: Before-and-after measurements of single case.

8. Productivity Results: Annual savings in costs reported as follows: supply, preparation and patient service, $137,082; cafeteria, $49,950; diet, $66,496. The elimination of 42 positions resulted in an additional savings of $263,438 per year.

9. Other Results: During program implementation, turnover virtually stopped and absenteeism dropped below 1%.

10. Intervening Effects: None reported.

*11. Limitations: A. Absence of control group.
               F. Single case.

1. Reference: Dettleback, W.W. & Kraft, P. Organization change through job enrichment. <u>Training and Development Journal</u>, 1971, <u>25</u>, 2-6.

2. Conclusions: Job enrichment appeared to result in increased quantity and quality of production, in reduced costs, and in improvement in job-related attitudes.*

3. Organization: Bankers Trust Company, a New York commercial bank.

4. Workers: Production typists who record stock-transfer data.

5. Program: Job enrichment to new modular design, which introduced into the job a number of related tasks and which increased responsibility for work done.

6. Method: Installed by management.

7. Design: Before-and-after measures of quantity and quality of production. Six months after the job-enrichment program was initiated, a random selection of 20% of the sample completed a job-attitude survey.

8. Productivity Results: After six months, production rates improved 92% in one section and more than 110% in two other sections. No increase in errors resulted when the checker job was eliminated.

9. Other Results: Job attitudes improved. Elimination of checkers for half the typists is reported to be saving the company $300,000 annually in salaries.

10. Intervening Effects: None reported.

*11. Limitations: A. Absence of control group.
                    F. Follow-up limited to six months.

1. Reference: Dowling, W. At GM: System 4 builds performance and profits. Organizational Dynamics, 1975, 3(3), 23-38.

2. Conclusions: Reorganization of worker and supervisory jobs, with increased worker participation and feedback, may result in increased
   efficiency and quality and decreased costs and grievances. These consequences do not occur in all instances, however.*

3. Organization: General Motors Lakewood plant, Atlanta, Georgia.

4. Workers: About 5,000 employees in plant, 250 in "cushion room."

5. Program: System redesign emphasizing increased employee participation:
   hourly employees received information about future products and about
   model changes, cost data, and labor cost comparisons with other plants;
   were asked for suggestions concerning new-model production changes;
   were given more than 20,000 hours of classroom training the first year.
   Training for salaried employees and for foreman candidates was increased. The foreman's job was redesigned by assignment of a "utility
   trainer" to help with non-supervisory functions. The "cushion room"
   was reorganized into cross-functional business teams; production and
   service functions were brought together in separate building, told to
   function as separate enterprise; employees participated in goal setting
   and in planning, and were given continued performance-feedback comparing the "cushion room" with other operations.

6. Method: Installed by management and consultants.

7. Design: Before-and-after measures for experimental groups only.

8. Productivity Results: 1969-1970 decrease in both indirect and direct
   labor efficiency. 1970-1971 decrease in indirect and increase in
   direct labor efficiency. 1971-1972 large increase in indirect and
   slight increase in direct labor efficiency. 1969 vs. 1972 10% improvement in monitored quality index and 60% decrease in grievances. "Cushion room": 1970-1971 decrease in written grievances and in scrap cost
   per unit.

9. Other Results: Supplemental findings in three other plants did not
   show expected improvement in systems and performance measures.

10. Intervening Effects: 1969-1970 improvement in organizational climate,
    supervisory and peer leadership, grand process and satisfactions (all
    via management-system questionnaire).

*11. Limitations: A. Absence of control group.
                   E. Initial low performance of plant; sympathetic plant
                      manager.
                   F. No tests of significance.

1. Reference: Doyle, F.P. Job enrichment plus OD--A two-pronged approach at Western Union. In J.R. Maher (ed.), New perspectives in job
enrichment. New York: Van Nostrand, Reinhold Co., 1971, pp. 193-205.

2. Conclusions: Job enrichment is credited with having reduced clerical
errors.*

3. Organization: Western Union, Philadelphia Bookkeeping Bureau.

4. Workers: Clerical workers.

5. Program: Over three phases, a job-restructure team composed of four
management and four union members changed the billing process. The 12
functions were no longer divided among different types of clerks, but
were shared among 12 bookkeeping clerks.

6. Method: Installed by management and union.

7. Design: Time-series measurements just prior to and during the job-enrichment program are reported.

8. Productivity Results: There was a reduction in percentage of filing
errors in relation to total message volume.

9. Other Results: None reported.

10. Intervening Effects: None reported.

*11. Limitations: A. Absence of control group
                   C. Criteria limited to percentage filing errors.
                   F. Small sample.
                   No tests of significance.

1. Reference: Driscoll, J.M., Meyer, R.G., & Schanie, C.F. Training police in family crisis intervention. Journal of Applied Behavioral
   Science, 1973, 9, 62-82.

2. Conclusions: An intensive multi-method training program for police
   officers, including supervision, appears to have improved the quality
   of their services.

3. Organization: Louisville, Kentucky police department.

4. Workers: 12 patrolmen on Louisville police force. Average age = 33
   years.

5. Program: Intensive training course to improve performance of police-
   men intervening in family crisis situations. Training included pres-
   entations, readings and films; simulations of family crisis interven-
   tions, with video replay and feedback; and supervised field interven-
   tions, in which teams answered at least one family-dispute call per
   evening. Six two-man crisis teams were formed of trained patrolmen.

6. Method: Installed by management.

7. Design: Post-training comparison of trained vs. untrained teams for a
   half year after completion of training course.

8. Productivity Results: Citizens dealt with by trained officers reported
   that they had more satisfaction with the intervention; that they had an
   increased regard for the police; that there was greater rapport between
   themselves and officers; and that there was greater involvement of
   officers.

9. Other Results: None reported.

10. Intervening Effects: During the course of the project, trained patrol-
    men reported heightened understanding of family problems; greater
    acceptance of patrolmen by citizens; greater receptivity to patrolmen's
    suggestions; a decrease in the use of force; and an increase in overall
    effectiveness.

11. Limitations: B. Equivalence of comparison groups questionable.
    F. Small sample.
    No tests of significance.

1. Reference: Dyer, E.D., Monson, M.A., & Cope, M.J. Increasing the
   quality of patient care through performance counseling and written goal
   setting. Nursing Research, 1975, 24, 138-144.

2. Conclusions: Allowing staff nurses to participate in setting written
   goals, while training their head nurses to provide them with positive
   feedback, may have a positive effect on short-term patient care.*

3. Organization: Seven Veterans' Administration hospitals matched and
   selected on basis of bed capacity, affiliations, patient turnover rates
   and geographic location; two located in South, two in Midwest, and
   three on West Coast; only medical and surgical wards.

4. Workers: 387 registered staff nurses from 60 wards; only 40% working
   on same ward with same head nurse by end of study; average age of
   staff nurses 42 years; 48% diploma, 14% associate degree, 30% bacca-
   laureate, 8% pursuing advanced degree.

5. Program: Participative management-by-objectives--including setting
   written goals, head nurse modeling, positive feedback. Done by
   training head nurses during two-day workshop to learn more about
   setting goals, as well as by providing opportunities for and reinforcement of staff nurses to achieve objectives. Goals set by head and
   staff nurses during performance-evaluation periods.

6. Method: Installed by management.

7. Design: Before-and-after measurements, with random assignment of 60
   wards to control and experimental conditions.

8. Productivity Results: After six months, experimental group had significantly higher mean scores on one of five scales of rated patient care;
   after 12 months, the control group was significantly higher on one of
   the scales. On another rating of patient care, no significant differences were found between the two groups, although the same trend
   appeared as on the other patient-care measure. After six months, four
   of six patient-interview responses were more positive for experimental
   group, one significantly more positive than for control; insignificant
   gains between six and 12 months on those four responses.

9. Other Results: After six months, experimental group showed significantly greater satisfaction on two out of four responses; between six
   and 12 months, experimental group showed greater satisfaction on three
   and less on two responses. Nurses with higher ratings in patient care
   gave more favorable descriptions of the hospital climate.

69

10. Intervening Effects: None reported.

*11. Limitations: C. Questionable sensitivity of patient-care measure
                      (observations for two to three hours by four R.N.'s).

1. Reference: Ely, D.D., & Morse, J.T. TA and reinforcement theory.
   Personnel, 1974, 51(2), 38-41.

2. Conclusions: Training managers in the understanding of human interaction, including the use of feedback, appears to reduce the rate at
   which workers under those managers resign. Replacement costs may
   therefore also be reduced.*

3. Organization: One of five geographical operating areas of General
   Telephone Company of the Southwest.

4. Workers: 96 managers representing all levels; 70 first- and second-
   level supervisors.

5. Program: Five-day training in transactional analysis and reinforcement.
   Included: (a) Introduction to TA as communications theory. (b) Con-
   tracts made for changes that supervisors want to see in themselves; informal group discussion and role playing of job interview (before TV
   camera, for purpose of video and group feedback). (c) Role playing of
   performance reviews and counseling of employees about work performance
   deficiencies (before TV). (d) Motivational theories. (e) Systems analysis theory. (f) Development of managerial actions and plans.

6. Method: Installed by management.

7. Design: Compared post-training measures of experimental group and of
   non-equivalent comparison group with pre-training measure of total
   sample.

8. Productivity Results: Compared to earlier resignation rate of .09 for
   total area, .03 rate for subordinates of trained managers was significantly lower, while that for untrained managers was .12. Savings in
   costs of training and processing replacement amounted to $46,000 for
   the experimental group.

9. Other Results: None reported.

10. Intervening Effects: None reported.

*11. Limitations: B. Non-equivalence of comparison groups.

1. Reference: Farr, J.L., O'Leary, B.S., & Bartlett, C.J. Effect of work
   sample test upon self-selection and turnover of job applicants. Journal
   of Applied Psychology, 1973, 58, 283-285.

2. Conclusions: A pre-employment work-sample test did not have the anticipated effect of reducing voluntary turnover.

3. Organization: Ladies' apparel factory located in mid-Atlantic state.

4. Workers: Female sewing-machine operators. Group A: N = 40, 16 white,
   24 black. Group B: N = 40, 15 white, 25 black. Group C: N = 80,
   36 white, 44 black.

5. Program: Pre-employment tests as a means of providing applicants with
   information about job requirements.

6. Method: Installed by management.

7. Design: Random assignment of subjects to experimental and control
   groups. Measures of voluntary turnover were obtained two, four and six
   weeks after employment. Group A received no tests; Group B received two
   tests not related to job; Group C received same two tests as B, plus a
   work-sample test.

8. Productivity Results: Voluntary turnover rates were essentially equal
   for all groups. White workers who had taken the work-sample test had
   somewhat less turnover than blacks.

9. Other Results: White applicants who had taken the work-sample test had
   higher job-refusal rate than blacks.

10 Intervening Effects: None reported.

11. Limitations: D. Job-related testing was limited in scope.
                  F. Small sample.

1. Reference: Favell, J.E. Reduction of staff tardiness by a feedback procedure. Proceedings, 81st Annual Convention, American Psychological Association, 1973, 893-894.

2. Conclusions: A feedback procedure may be useful in reducing tardiness.*

3. Organization: Institution for retarded children.

4. Workers: Six members of an administrative committee, and a secretary.

5. Program: Feedback procedure to increase punctual arrival of participants at staff meetings. Each individual was able to compare his own performance with that of others attending the meetings, as well as to compare his past performance with his present performance.

6. Method: Installed by a committee member.

7. Design: Before-and-after measurements of experimental group only.

8. Productivity Results: Initially, during sessions when feedback was given, meetings started more promptly, more members arrived on time, and less time was spent waiting by others. These effects decreased over time, but did not revert entirely to pre-intervention levels.

9. Other Results: None reported.

10. Intervening Effects: None reported.

*11. Limitations: A. Absence of control group.
                     F. Small sample.
                        No tests of significance.

DOT: 20   #22
SIC: E-481
Program: 8,9
Criterion: 1,2,5,6

1. Reference: Ford, R. Job enrichment lessons from AT&T. Harvard Business Review, 1973, 51, 96-106.

2. Conclusions: In various situations, the enrichment of individual jobs and the use of job nesting are described as having improved production rates, turnover rates, and absence rates.*

3. Organization: Various companies within the Bell system.

4. Workers: Employees below supervisory level.

5. Program: Individual jobs were enriched through systematic changes in the module of work, through control of the module, and through feedback indicating what was accomplished. The enrichment program also included reorganizing the work of groups beyond individual jobs (called "nesting").

6. Method: Installed by management.

7. Design: Productivity results attributable to the job-enrichment strategy and to job nesting are illustrated.

8. Productivity Results: (a) In one company, a 50% improvement in turnover is reported as attributable to enrichment of individual jobs. (b) Where job nesting was used in another company, number of orders typed on time increased from 27% to 100% a half year later. (c) Where job nesting was used in a third company, the number of service order pages were typed at a rate one third higher than in a comparison group. (d) Absenteeism in an experimental unit was 0.6% as compared to 2.5%, and errors per 100 orders was 2.9, compared with 4.6 in a comparison group.

9. Other Results: None reported.

10. Intervening Effects: None reported.

*11. Limitations: Since there was a lack of specificity, any of the following defects may apply--
    A. and B. Comparison groups sometimes absent or non-equivalent.
    E. Illustrations may not have been representative of all enrichment experiments conducted.
    F. No tests of significance.

74

1. Reference: Frank, L.L. & Hackman, J.R. A failure of job enrichment: The case of the change that wasn't. <u>Journal of Applied Behavioral Science</u>, 1975, <u>11</u>, 413-436.

2. Conclusions: Numerous factors internal and external to a job-enrichment program can act to limit its effects and can lead to insignificant productivity results.*

3. Organization: A large metropolitan bank.

4. Workers: Stock-transfer department with 300 employees performing 16 functions. Program involved employees performing the six most central jobs: preparation clerk, processor, operator, legal clerk, correction clerk, and typist. 85% were female; mean age 33 years; modal high school education.

5. Program: Two group modules, each acting as a semiautonomous workgroup with its own supervisor and with complete responsibility for a specific group of corporations. Eight to 12 employees were in each module, were to be trained in all functions, and reported to a work coordinator (first-line supervisor). Enriching tasks were added, with several feedback mechanisms.

6. Method: Installed by management, personnel department and consultants.

7. Design: Measurements were obtained after the program was installed, and were compared with those for non-equivalent control groups; for one of the experimental groups, before-and-after measurements were obtained.

8. Productivity Results: No significant differences were found for the performance-quality ratings by supervisors or for absence data.

9. Other Results: On satisfaction or work motivation measures, no significant differences were found between groups.

10. Intervening Effects: Most job-core perceptions were significantly higher in experimental than in comparison groups. Significant positive correlations were found between the job-core perceptions and several satisfaction measures.

*11. Limitations: B. Non-equivalence of comparison groups.
                   D. No cross-training; feedback/computer problems; temporary replacement of executive V.P.; weak module boundaries; expiration of consultant contract; responsibility still retained by management; interpersonal problems.
                   F. Small sample.

DOT: unspecified
SIC: D-323
Program: 14
Criterion: 1,3,6,7

1. Reference: Glaser, E.M. Improving the quality of worklife ... And in the process, improving productivity. Los Angeles: Human Interaction Research Institute, 1974, pp. 53-56.

2. Conclusions: Various improvements in productivity occurred at Donnelly Mirrors, Inc., over a 20-year period, during which a number of major changes were made in the work system.*

3. Organization: Donnelly Mirrors, Inc., Holland, Michigan.

4. Workers: 600 employees.

5. Program: (a) From 1953 to present, version of the Scanlon Plan. (b) From 1967, participative management program, with small work teams taking on these responsibilities: selection of new team members and supervisors; handling of discipline; and development of goals, work strategies, and solutions to problems. Supervisor of team was also a member of the next highest team. (c) From 1970, hourly employees were put on salary, and pay increases were determined by a committee that included employees.

6. Method: Installed by management and consultants.

7. Design: Case study, with before-and-after measures.

8. Productivity Results: Company estimated that over 20 years, productivity doubled. From 1968 to 1973, quality-control personnel decreased from 14 to 4. Absenteeism decreased from 5% to $1\frac{1}{2}$%. Tardiness fell from 6% to less than 1%. Turnover was negligible. From 1953 to present, compound growth rate was 14%, and return on investment tripled.

9. Other Results: None reported.

10. Intervening Effects: None reported.

*11. Limitations: A. Absence of control group.
                     E. Small, non-union firm; small town.
                     F. No tests of significance.

1. Reference: Glaser, E.M. <u>Improving the quality of worklife ... And in the process, improving productivity.</u> Los Angeles: Human Interaction Research Institute, 1974, pp. 106-112.

2. Conclusions: Following the redesign of jobs, productivity improved.*

3. Organization: A plant of General Electric Company.

4. Workers: Manufacturing, shop-floor operators.

5. Program: Job redesign: increased employee involvement (stewardship); modification of assembly process so that one operator could follow unit down line. Role-playing program to give employees better understanding of manufacturing process. Employees given feedback of total output required of and achieved by unit.

6. Method: Installed by management.

7. Design: Before-and-after measures of experimental group only.

8. Productivity Results: Defects-per-operator reduced about 50%. Output rose from an average of 25.7 units for nine months before programs to an average of 46.7 units after. Before assembly changes, output averaged 40 units per month; but it increased to 52 units one month after, 60 units two months after, and 71 units three months after changes. In the department with hourly semi-skilled equipment operators, the introduction of self-inspection reduced cost due to product failures by about 25% during the first year.

9. Other Results: None reported.

10. Intervening Effects: None reported.

*11. Limitations: A. Absence of control group.
                    F. No tests of significance.

1. Reference: Glaser, E.M. <u>Improving the quality of worklife ... And in</u>
   <u>the process, improving productivity.</u> Los Angeles: Human Interaction
   Research Institute, 1974, pp. 124-129.

2. Conclusions: Productivity, turnover, and attendance improved after
   problem-solving teams were formed.*

3. Organization: Communications Division, Motorola Corporation.

4. Workers: Various employees (e.g., technicians assembling, testing and
   packing radio pocket-pagers; new line of operators building receivers).

5. Program: Team problem-solving program: teams of workers electing own
   captain and setting own goals (e.g., problem-solving team formed of
   ten female operators trying to build receiver).

6. Method: Installed by management.

7. Design: Before-and-after measures of experimental group only.

8. Productivity Results: Team-program results: production output improved more than 30%; after six months, turnover decreased on an average of 25%; rejects decreased from 30-40 per month to a negligible
   amount; attendance increased to about 95%.

9. Other Results: None reported.

10. Intervening Effects: None reported.

*11. Limitations: A. Absence of control group.
                   F. No tests of significance.

1. Reference: Goldstein, A.P. & Sorcher, M. <u>Changing supervisor behavior.</u>
   New York: Pergamon Press, 1974, pp. 70-73.

2. Conclusions: Voluntary turnover rate seems to decrease when male black
   employees with hard-core-unemployed backgrounds and their supervisors
   are trained to model behaviors that are adaptive to the work environment.*

3. Organization: Two geographical locations of unspecified company.

4. Workers: 20 male, black, hard-core-unemployed employees in experimental group and 19 in comparison group; unspecified number of supervisors..

5. Program: Parallel modeling programs for hard-core-unemployed black employees and for their supervisors: five filmed incidents presented to
   employees and five similar situations to supervisors as examples of
   effective model behavior; incidents obtained via interviews with hard-
   core-unemployed black employees concerning their problems and with
   foremen concerning theirs; high-status narrators used (e.g., plant
   manager for supervisors, black athlete for employees); followed by discussion and by role playing of similar situations.

6. Method: Installed by management and consultants.

7. Design: Non-equivalent comparison group.

8. Productivity Results: Six months after training, voluntary quit rate
   was almost three times higher for workers in comparison than for
   workers in experimental group.

9. Other Results: Supervisors were said to be very enthusiastic about new-
   employee performance.

10. Intervening Effects: Trained employees commented that program enabled
    them to handle themselves better in situations they before had thought
    threatening.

*11. Limitations: B. Non-equivalence of comparison groups.
                   E. Small and possibly unrepresentative sample.
                   F. No tests of significance.

1. Reference: Goldstein, A.P. & Sorcher, M. Changing supervisor behavior. New York: Pergamon Press, 1974, pp. 73-82.

2. Conclusions: Workers supervised by foremen who have gone through an "applied learning" training program featuring the modeling of effective behavior are more efficient than are workers supervised by foremen who have gone through a "traditional" training program.

3. Organization: A manufacturing plant.

4. Workers: First-level supervisors (foremen).

5. Program: Applied Learning: training consisting of ten two-hour sessions in which model behavior is presented on film, followed by discussion and role-playing of similar situations. Traditional Training: lectures, discussions, unstructured role-playing. Second- and third-level managers had been trained previously. A pilot study was done in another plant.

6. Method: Installed by management and by consultants.

7. Design: Ten foremen in Applied Learning group and ten in Traditional Training group. Analysis of the performance of about 200 workers reporting to above foremen, with time-series measures for ten weeks prior to and ten weeks after training.

8. Productivity Results: Level of productive efficiency (actual vs. estimated standard production) was significantly higher for workers supervised by foremen trained in Applied Learning program than for workers supervised by those traditionally trained.

9. Other Results: A pilot study done in another plant involved the training of eight foremen; it was followed by an average decrease of 15% in unapplied direct labor (consisting of idle time, scrap, rework, etc.).

10. Intervening Effects: None reported.

11. Limitations: B. Non-equivalence of comparison groups.

DOT: 18,unspecified   #29
SIC: unspecified
Program: 13
Criterion: 3,5,6,15

1. Reference: Golembiewski, R.T., Hilles, R. & Kagno, M.S. A longitudinal study of flexi-time effects: Some consequences of an OD structural intervention. Journal of Applied Behavioral Science, 1974, 10, 503-532.

2. Conclusions: A program of flexible work hours resulted in decreased absenteeism (total days absent) and in more favorable attitudes toward work, but did not affect turnover.*

3. Organization: Three units at one Research and Development field site, each representing a different scientific discipline.

4. Workers: Experimental Unit A (12 employees, 5 managers); Experimental Unit B (20 employees, 6 managers); Comparison Unit (18 employees, 4 managers). Different comparison group for absenteeism/turnover data (N not given; differed from experimental units on these outcome measures before program).

5. Program: Flexible working hours during 35-hour week: flexible time between 7:00 a.m. and 9:15 a.m.; five-hour fixed core period between 9:15 a.m. and 3:00 p.m. (excluding 45-minute fixed lunch period); another flexible period between 3:00 p.m. and 6:00 p.m. Minimum workday of five hours (core); time clock used for experimental units' weekly-roll employees and semi-monthly employees time sheet used for comparison unit's semi-monthly employees.

6. Method: Installed by management and consultants.

7. Design: Multiple time-series measures of three units' employee and managerial attitudes, taken two weeks before and on day of installation, and again six months and then one year after installation. Productivity measures taken for periods one year before and after program.

8. Productivity Results: Experimental units down 35% in total paid days absent; comparison group up 15.2%. Contrary to expectation, experimental units up 12.7% in single-day-or-less absent; comparison group up 12%. 15% decrease in average number of support personnel; 12% decrease in cost of all support services (no data for comparison group).

9. Other Results: General improvement in job attitudes of two experimental units, comparing pretest with surveys 6 and 12 months later. Some deterioration of attitudes in comparison unit. Greater immediate improvement (i.e., after six months) for workers than for managers. (For factor analysis of attitudinal data, see Golembiewski. R.T., Yeager, S. & Hilles, R. Factor analysis of some flexi-time effects: Attitudinal and behavioral consequences of a structural intervention. Academy of Management Journal, 1975, 18, 500-509.)

10. Intervening Effects: Pattern seemed to be to work later one day and leave earlier on another.

*11. Limitations: B. Non-equivalence of comparison groups.
                   E. R & D site; culture favoring organization development.
                   F. No tests of significance.

1. Reference: Gomez, L.R. & Mussie, S.J. An application of job enrichment in a civil service setting: A demonstration study. Public
   Personnel Management, 1975, 4, 49-54.

2. Conclusions: Job enrichment may improve job performance and satisfaction, but not change absenteeism.*

3. Organization: Selection division of Midwestern city's personnel department.

4. Workers: Eight female clerical workers; ages from 21 to 60 years,
   average of 31; average 12 years, 3 months formal education; one year,
   four months tenure in present job; and six years in present occupation.

5. Program: Change from fractionated to self-contained unit system;
   changes were made through training sessions and through procedural and
   physical rearrangements.

6. Method: Installed by management, with implementation by teams of
   workers.

7. Design: Before-and-after measures of experimental group only.

8. Productivity Results: Significant improvement in all eight mean supervisory ratings of job performance. No significant change in
   absenteeism.

9. Other Results: Statistically significant increase in mean job satisfaction.

10. Intervening Effects: None reported.

*11. Limitations: A. Absence of control group.
                   C. Performance measured by ratings, which may have been
                      affected by raters' knowledge of changes.
                   E. Small and possibly unrepresentative sample.

DOT: 070,075,187,195,201   #31
SIC: I-806
Program: 13
Criterion: 1,6

1. Reference: Greene, J.A. Restructuring staff time: The 8-day week.
   Hospital and Community Psychiatry, 1974, 25, 733-735.

2. Conclusions: A work schedule consisting of eight ten-hour days followed
   by six days off appears to have had favorable effects in psychiatric
   facilities.*

3. Organization: Psychiatry Associates, a private psychiatric practice,
   and Hill Crest Hospital, private psychiatric, average 80 patients
   (Birmingham, Alabama).

4. Workers: Psychiatry Associates: professional staff of five psychiatrists, one clinical psychologist, and one social worker; office staff.
   Hospital: six full-time psychiatrists, one part-time psychiatrist, two
   psychiatric residents, social work and activity-therapy staff, nursing
   staff, supervisory personnel.

5. Program: Schedule of eight-day week: ten hours a day for eight consecutive days, followed by six days off (8/6 schedule); teams formed, each
   with two psychiatrists, two social workers and two adjunctive thera-
   pists; one-half of team working eight days while other half off for six
   days.

6. Method: Installed by staff.

7. Design: Two six-week trial periods separated by two-and-a-half-month
   resumption of working five days and having two days off (5/2 schedule).
   Before-and-after measures of experimental groups only, with measures
   taken for 1½ years afterwards.

8. Productivity Results: Length of patient-stay in hospital was 20% less
   under 8/6 than under 5/2 schedule. Cost per stay under 8/6 schedule
   was $1,631 compared to $2,121 under 5/2. Absenteeism under 8/6 was less
   than one day per person, compared to four days per person under 5/2.

9. Other Results: None reported.

10. Intervening Effects: After six months, 67% of staff rated 8/6 as
    superior, 25% as inferior, and 8% as equal to 5/2. After ten months,
    56.5% of patients discharged since adoption of schedule preferred 8/6,
    14.5% preferred 5/2, and 29% expressed no preference.

*11. Limitations: A. Absence of control group.
                   F. Small sample.
                   No tests of significance.

1. Reference: Hand, H.H. & Slocum, J.W., Jr. A longitudinal study of the
   effects of a human relations training program on managerial effectiveness. <u>Journal of Applied Psychology</u>, 1972, <u>56</u>, 412-417. (See also
   Abstract No. 33.)

2. Conclusions: An intensive training program in human relations appears
   to have induced managers to have more positive attitudes toward the
   human dimensions of their jobs, and to have resulted in their receiving
   higher performance-ratings from supervisors.*

3. Organization: Specialty-steel plant in central Pennsylvania.

4. Workers: 21 line and staff managers for experimental and control
   groups.

5. Program: Human relations training program designed to provide application of human relations principles through various problem-solving
   methods. Phase 1 emphasized discussion of managerial styles. Phase 2
   dealt with experimental learning and included, among other exercises,
   self-ratings on the managerial grid, and an in-basket exercise. Phase
   3 was devoted to motivation theories.

6. Method: Installed by management.

7. Design: Random assignment of managers to experimental and control
   groups, with before-and-after measures. Post-test measures taken 18
   months after completion of training.

8. Productivity Results: Subjects in the experimental group improved
   significantly in performance, as rated by their superiors. The control
   group was rated as having become significantly less effective.

9. Other Results: None.

10. Intervening Effects: The experimental group developed more-positive
    attitudes toward human relations factors in their jobs; these attitudes
    were correlated with the positive changes in job performance.

*11. Limitations: C. Performance measures consisted of ratings, which were
                      possibly influenced by raters' awareness of who was
                      trained.
                   E. Small and possibly unrepresentative sample.

1. Reference: Hand, H., Richards, M. and Slocum, R. Organizational climate and the effectiveness of a human relations training program.
   <u>Academy of Management Journal</u>, 1973, <u>16</u>, 185-195. (See also Abstract
   No. 32.)

2. Conclusions: Training in human relations appears to have improved rated
   performance as well as attitudes of managers who perceived themselves to
   be in a consultative climate, but not of those who perceived an autocratic climate.*

3. Organization: Steel plant in central Pennsylvania.

4. Workers: Line and staff managers; 21 in experimental and 21 in control
   group.

5. Program: Human relations training program intended to change managerial
   attitudes and effectiveness.

6. Method: Installed by management.

7. Design: Random assignment to experimental and control groups, which
   were then subdivided according to perceived organizational climate
   (consultative vs. autocratic). Measures were taken 90 days and again 18
   months after training.

8. Productivity Results: In the experimental group, managers who reported
   working in a consultative climate showed a significant increase in performance, as rated by superiors; rated performance did not change for
   those in an autocratic climate. In the control group, rated performance
   declined, regardless of climate.

9. Other Results: 90 days after completion of program, there were no significant changes in attitudes: 18 months later, however, there was in
   the experimental group an increase in managerial concern for human relations, and in the control group, a decrease. Top management is also
   reported to have given greater salary increases and managerial promo-
   tions to managers in the experimental and control groups who reported a
   consultative climate.

10. Intervening Effects: None.

*11. Limitations: C. Performance measured by ratings, possibly affected by
                   raters' awareness of who was trained.

DOT: 195   #34
SIC: J-944
Program: 14
Criterion: 1,2,3

1. Reference: Harris, K.L. Organizing to overhaul a mess. California
   Management Review, 1975, 17(3), 40-49. (See also Abstract No. 93.)

2. Conclusions: Extensive changes in management and in organization improved the performance of a municipal welfare system that had been
   beset by numerous problems.*

3. Organization: Human Resources Administration of New York City.

4. Workers: 27,000 employees in New York City's welfare centers.

5. Program: Overhaul of welfare system, mainly by replacement of managers,
   increase in monitoring and in central control, and tough discipline
   program.

6. Method: Installed by management; using project management organization,
   consisting of from 70 to 300 professionals plus consultants, that
   designed and implemented the plan and was then dissolved after 1½ years.

7. Design: Before-and-after measures of experimental group only.

8. Productivity Results: 16% increase in employee productivity; error rate
   decline from 35% to 15%; bottom-line reversal in size of welfare rolls,
   ending in a steady decline (removed 13,000 from rolls); 15% increase in
   rejection rate of welfare applicants; backlog in cases reduced by
   115,000.

9. Other Results: None reported.

10. Intervening Effects: None reported.

*11. Limitations: A. Absence of control group.
                    E. Extreme number of problems at outset.

1. Reference: Hautaluoma, J.E. & Gavin, J.F. Effects of organizational
   diagnosis and intervention on blue-collar "blues." Journal of Applied
   Behavioral Science, 1975, 11, 475-498.

2. Conclusions: At least in the short haul, an intervention including
   organizational diagnosis, feedback, and supervisory/management workshops
   appears to improve employee satisfaction, but the intervention's effects
   on turnover and absenteeism are less clearcut.*

3. Organization: Small lumber company.

4. Workers: In major division, 70 workers described as having morale problems; 10 managerial, 11 clerical and 48 blue-collar/shop employees. Involved in assembly of prefabricated units used in building construction;
   work consisted of simplified, short-cycle tasks by crews of five, with
   distinct hierarchy of job functions.

5. Program: (a) Diagnosis by general meeting, discussion with blue-collar
   employees, general interviews, and job-attitudes questionnaire. (b)
   Data-feedback meetings two weeks later, first with management and clerical groups, then more general; homogeneous managerial, clerical and
   blue-collar worker subgroups for discussion of what to do about feedback;
   management-group meeting for specific decision making. (c) Management-
   team-development workshop away from plant. (d) First-line supervisory-
   skills workshop, with some blue-collar workers, for introduction to
   alternatives in methods of supervision of production; questionnaire,
   feedback, and discussion of supervisors' and blue-collar workers'
   attitudes about actual and desired supervisory styles, with lectures,
   discussions, films, and role playing of critical incidents that were
   videotaped and discussed.

6. Method: Installed by management, personnel department, and consultants.

7. Design: Action research, involving before-, during-, and after-measures
   of experimental group only, latter taken three months after intervention.

8. Productivity Results: Insignificant change in overall turnover, but reduced for older employees. Absenteeism rate was reduced (8.65% to
   5.88%).

9. Other Results: For blue-collar and all employees, job attitudes showed
   significant improvement in psychological meaning of job; significant
   increase in satisfaction with supervision; significant increase in satisfaction with pay and promotion; significant increase in overall satisfaction.

10. Intervening Effects: None reported.

*11. Limitations: A. Absence of control group.
                    C. Post-intervention measures taken only three months
                       later.
                    E. Initially, high turnover and absenteeism, low morale.

DOT: 189
SIC: I-822
Program: 4,10
Criterion: 2

1. Reference: Hegarty, W.H. Using subordinate ratings to elicit behavioral changes in supervisors. Journal of Applied Psychology, 1974, 6, 764-766.

2. Conclusions: Improvements in subordinate-rated supervisory behavior may occur when supervisors are told how they were rated earlier by their subordinates.*

3. Organization: University of North Carolina.

4. Workers: 56 first-line supervisors of University staff employees; 13 departments involved.

5. Program: Supervisors given feedback of subordinate ratings on 15 specific behaviors and on 1 item measuring overall performance; 60 to 90 minutes spent going over individual reports.

6. Method: Installed by management and consultant.

7. Design: Experimental vs. control group design; random assignment of supervisors to two groups, with ratings taken two weeks before and again ten weeks after experimental group was given feedback reports.

8. Productivity Results: Experimental group significantly superior to control on all 15 post-feedback ratings and on summary item; no pretest differences.

9. Other Results: None reported.

10. Intervening Effects: None reported.

*11. Limitations: C. Performance results limited to ratings with measures taken only ten weeks after intervention.

1. Reference: Herzberg, F.I. & Rafalko, E.A. Efficiency in the military:
   Cutting costs with orthodox job enrichment. Personnel, 1975, 52(6),
   38-48.

2. Conclusions: Installation of various job-enrichment programs was
   followed by increased production efficiency and/or quality.*

3. Organization: Ogden Air Logistics Center at Hill Air Force Base.

4. Workers: Over 1,000 employees in wide variety of jobs; over 260 supervisors.

5. Program: Five divisions had key men participate in three-week training
   program; they selected pilot projects in own functional areas and acted
   as internal consultants, working with supervisors. Four projects are
   described: (a) Avionics (flight-line and production-line technicians
   consolidated); (b) Wing Slat (total aircraft job assigned to crews with
   direct-contact mechanics and quality inspectors); (c) Installation
   Division (more responsibility given to warehousemen/drivers); (d) Magnetic Tape Library (responsibility was increased).

6. Method: Installed by management and consultants.

7. Design: Before-and-after measures of experimental groups; in one project, comparison group involved.

8. Productivity Results: (a) Avionics: test flights were reduced by
   about half, with estimated $85,648 savings. (b) Wing Slat: experi-
   mental group surpassed non-equivalent comparison group, with more than
   $89,000 savings. (c) Installation Division: inspection function was
   eliminated, with $37,000 savings; 90% improvement in service, via
   customer-satisfaction survey. (d) Magnetic Tape Library: average
   number of lost tapes decreased from nine to one per month, with $4,216
   savings. Total savings for 11 projects from April 1974 to January 1975
   was $264,549.

9. Other Results: None reported.

10. Intervening Effects: None reported.

*11. Limitations: A. and B. Absence of control or of equivalent comparison
                   groups.
                E. Illustrative cases may not be representative of all
                   experiments.
                F. No tests of significance.

DOT: 184
SIC: E-42
Program: 3,10
Criterion: 1,2

#38

1. Reference: Holder, J., Jr. Evaluation of an in-company management training program. <u>Training and Development Journal</u>, 1971, <u>26</u>(4), 24-27.

2. Conclusions: Training of first-line supervisors may result in improvement in on-the-job behaviors of participants and improvement in the performance of departments supervised by them.*

3. Organization: Yellow Freight System, Inc., Kansas City, Mo.

4. Workers: 600 supervisors located throughout 100 terminals in 30 states.

5. Program: One-day training meetings for supervisors and branch managers. Attention was given to order giving, performance appraisal, prevention and handling of grievances, decision making, and initiation of change.

6. Method: Installed by management.

7. Design: Six months after conclusion of training meetings, terminal supervisors were asked to evaluate their own on-the-job behavior and attitudes in the areas covered at the meetings. At the same time, branch managers were asked to rate supervisors' behavior and attitudes. Supervisors and branch managers also evaluated changes in nonsupervisory employees who were under supervisors' direction.

8. Productivity Results: After attendance in the program, 77.1% of supervisors reported an improvement in the quality of production of their departments. 68.5% indicated that quantity of production had improved. There were few reports of declines. 74.6% of branch managers reported improvement in quality of production; 61.4% of branch managers indicated that quantity of production had improved.

9. Other Results: None reported.

10. Intervening Effects: Significant improvement by supervisors in the areas of order giving, decision making, training, and attitude toward the job.

*11. Limitations: A. Absence of control groups.
                   C. Ratings as performance criteria; may be affected by raters' awareness that training had occurred.
                   F. No tests of significance.

DOT: 7-unspecified   #39
SIC: D-unspecified, D-35,D-284,D-386,D-391
Program: 7
Criterion: 3,6

1. Reference: Hulme, R.D. & Bevan, R.V. The blue-collar worker goes on salary. Harvard Business Review, 1975, 53(2), 104-112.

2. Conclusions: For blue-collar workers in five companies, changing from hourly pay to weekly salaries increased average absenteeism.*

3. Organization: Gillette Company Safety Razor Division in Boston, Massachusetts; Polaroid Corporation in Cambridge, Massachusetts; Kinetic Dispersion Corporation in Buffalo, New York; Avon Products in New York, New York; Black and Decker Manufacturing Company in Towson, Maryland.

4. Workers: Various blue-collar employees of above companies; non-union except for Kinetic Dispersion (United Auto Workers).

5. Program: Introduction of weekly salary plans in lieu of hourly rate. Gillette (1955), Polaroid (1966), Kinetic (1962), Avon (1972), Black and Decker (1971).

6. Method: Installed by management and union (Kinetic).

7. Design: Before-and-after measures of experimental groups only.

8. Productivity Results: Absenteeism rate increased by an average of 15%. Incremental cost amounts to about 1% of the payroll.

9. Other Results: Impressions of attitudes.

10. Intervening Effects: None reported.

*11. Limitations: A. Absence of control groups.
                   C. Bases for absenteeism rate not specified, or not comparable between companies.
                   F. No tests of significance.

DOT: 72,281
SIC: D-36
Program: 5
Criterion: 1,2,6,12

1. Reference: Ivancevich, J.M. Changes in performance in a management by objectives program. Administrative Science Quarterly, 1974, 19, 563-574.

2. Conclusions: A plant-wide management-by-objectives (MBO) program generally improves performance of production workers and of salesmen, although grievances may increase. Adding a program of verbal reinforcement relating to attainment of objectives further improves performance.

3. Organization: Three of six plants in the Palos Manufacturing Corporation, which produces electrical products and machine parts, for industry.

4. Workers: Line workers from the production department and salesmen from the marketing department; unionized. Four levels of management; number of first-line supervisors ranged from 21 to 42; education from 12 to 15 years; average span of control from 12 to 18 employees.

5. Program: MBO plus reinforcement. (a) MBO program installed in two experimental plants (E1, E2): four-day training session for entire management group, with next year's objective prepared by top-level management and distributed to middle and lower levels of management. (b) Reinforcement program added in E2: variable reinforcement of MBO program by top-level operating committee via letters, meetings, memos, telephone discussions; instituted about 21 months after implementation of MBO as above.

6. Method: Installed by top management, personnel department, and consultant.

7. Design: Multiple time-series measures in E1, E2, and comparison plant (C): data collection 12 months before MBO implementation, at point of implementation, and 6 months, 18 months, and 24 months after implementation. Measures of performance quantity and quality, absenteeism, and grievances in production department; measures of quantitative sales performance in marketing department.

8. Productivity Results: Production department: 6 months after implementation, production quantity and quality and absenteeism were on the average significantly improved in E1, quantity in E2, while no measures improved in C; grievance rate increased significantly in E1 and C; 24 months after implementation, quantity, quality and absenteeism were significantly improved in E2, while no measures showed improvement in E1 and C; significantly higher grievance rate was maintained in E1 and C. Marketing department: 6 months after implementation, there were significant improvements in three aspects of sales performance in E1 and E2, none in C; 24 months after implementation, there were three

significant improvements only in E2. For period of reinforcement program in E2, there were significant improvements in production quantity, absenteeism and grievance rate in the production department, and later in two sales performance measures in the marketing department.

9. Other Results: None reported.

10. Intervening Effects: None reported.

11. Limitations: B. Equivalence of comparison groups questionable.
    D. Short duration of reinforcement program.

DOT: 826
SIC: D-356
Program: 13
Criterion: 2,6,15

1. Reference: Ivancevich, J.M. Effects of the shorter workweek on se-lected satisfaction and performance measures. Journal of Applied Psychology, 1974, 59, 717-721.

2. Conclusions: A change in the workweek to a 4/40 schedule results in improvement in certain ratings of performance as well as in attitudes, but without affecting absenteeism.

3. Organization: Company that designs, manufactures, and markets a packaging machine.

4. Workers: Operating employees; 104 in the experimental group and 106 in the comparison group.

5. Program: Conversion from a 5-day, 40-hour workweek to a 4-day, 40-hour workweek.

6. Method: Installed by management.

7. Design: Before-and-after measures of experimental and comparison groups, with measures taken 1 month before change, and again 3 months and then 12 months after change.

8. Productivity Results: For three out of five performance facets, ex-perimental group improved significantly in supervisory ratings; in comparison group, no significant changes. For both groups, no signi-ficant change in absenteeism rate.

9. Other Results: Experimental group showed a small but statistically significant improvement in overall job satisfaction and in perceived anxiety stress.

10. Intervening Effects: None reported.

11. Limitations: B. Non-equivalence of comparison groups.
                   C. Performance ratings may have been affected by raters' knowledge of change.

DOT: 203
SIC: E-481
Program: 8
Criterion: 1,2

1. Reference: Janson, R. Job enrichment in the modern office. In J.R. Maher (ed.), <u>New perspectives in job enrichment</u>. New York: Van Nostrand, Reinhold, 1971, pp. 91-112.

2. Conclusions: Job enrichment improved quantity and quality of performance, as well as job attitudes.

3. Organization: The Bell system.

4. Workers: Production typists; 40 in the experimental group and 40 in the control group.

5. Program: Through a workshop, changes in job design were introduced. These included: (a) Typing work would not be externally verified, and typists would correct their own mistakes. (b) Typists would change their own tapes. (c) Feedback would be given by checkers rather than by supervisors. (d) Typists would be responsible for all typing for companies assigned to them.

6. Method: Installed by management.

7. Design: Workers were assigned to experimental and control groups. Measures were taken at the time of the workshop and then again a half year later.

8. Productivity Results: In the experimental group, hourly output increased by approximately 20%, while the control group remained constant. For the experimental group, errors per week decreased by about 70%, but not for the control group.

9. Other Results: Job attitudes improved in the experimental group, but showed a downward trend in the control group.

10. Intervening Effects: None reported.

11. Limitations: F. No tests of significance.

DOT: 210
SIC: E-481
Program: 8
Criterion: 2,5   #43

1. Reference: Janson, R. Job enrichment in the modern office. In
   J.R. Maher (ed.), New perspectives in job enrichment. New York:
   Van Nostrand, Reinhold, 1971, pp. 91-112.

2. Conclusions: Job enrichment appears to have improved work quality,
   turnover, and attitudes.*

3. Organization: The Bell system.

4. Workers: Auditing clerks; 18 in experimental group and 16 in control
   group.

5. Program: A two-day workshop was conducted, as a result of which what
   was originally accomplished as three separate functions was collapsed
   into one job. Clerks dealt with whole companies instead of with
   special fragments of work; decided whether their work should be verified; and dealt with other departments and with problem cases formerly
   handled by supervisors.

6. Method: Installed by management.

7. Design: Workers were assigned to experimental and control groups.
   Measures were taken for one-half year after the program was installed.

8. Productivity Results: Six months after initiation of the program, the
   number of errors made by the experimental group were less than 20% of
   the number made by the control group. In the experimental group,
   turnover was 15% below that in the control group.

9. Other Results: Job attitudes improved in experimental group, but not
   in control group.

10. Intervening Effects: None reported.

*11. Limitations: B. Possible lack of comparability of groups.
                    F. No tests of significance.

DOT: 213   #44
SIC: H-631
Program: 8
Criterion: 1,2,3,5,6,15

1. Reference: Janson, R. <u>Job enrichment trial--Data processing depart-</u>
   <u>ment analysis and results in an insurance organization</u>. Paper presented at the International Conference on the Quality of Working Life,
   Arden House, Harriman, New York, September 1972. Cited in E.M. Glaser,
   <u>Improving the quality of worklife ... And in the process, improving</u>
   <u>productivity</u>. Los Angeles: Human Interaction Research Institute,
   1974, pp. 115-123.

2. Conclusions: Following the enrichment of keypunch operators' jobs,
   the rate and quality of production, as well as absenteeism and job
   attitudes, improved. On the other hand, turnover increased. Substantial cost savings was estimated to result.*

3. Organization: Large insurance company.

4. Workers: 40 keypunch operators in the experimental group. Also, a
   comparison group.

5. Program: Job enrichment: 25 changes, which included operators' being
   more responsible for their own work; correcting obvious coding errors
   and own errors; and dealing directly with customers.

6. Method: Installed by management.

7. Design: Before-and-after measures of experimental and comparison
   groups.

8. Productivity Results: Productivity ratio 104% in experimental group
   and 94% in comparison. Throughput rate nine months after initiation of
   program was 39.6% in experimental and 8.1% in comparison. Effectiveness ratio (hours to complete given number cards/standard) increased
   26% in experimental group. Error rate decreased 35.3% in experimental group (from 1.53% to 1%) and 8% in comparison. For ratings of
   keypunch accuracy, operators receiving an "outstanding" rating increased from 20% to 50%, and operators receiving a poor rating decreased from 11.1% to 5.5% (no comparison data). Experimental-group
   absenteeism improved by 24%, while comparison-group absenteeism increased 29%. Turnover increased 6.4% in experimental and decreased
   5.1% in comparison. Savings calculated at $64,305.

9. Other Results: On a job-attitude survey, experimental-group scores increased over 11 months 16.5% for the 9 job factors, while comparison-
   group attitudes remained the same.

10. Intervening Effects: None reported.

*11. Limitations: B. Non-equivalence of comparison groups.
                   F. No tests of significance.

                               99

1. Reference: Johnson, R.J. Problem resolution and imposition of change through a participative group effort. <u>Journal of Management Studies</u>, 1974, <u>11</u>, 129-142.

2. Conclusions: A lower-level coordinating group's participation in devising changes in operations may decrease delays in the processing of orders.*

3. Organization: Special Services Division of a telephone company.

4. Workers: Mainly "paper-moving" functions, such as WATS line service, answering services, computer connections, other specialized uses of telephone circuits.

5. Program: Representatives from each work group formed a coordinating task force to discuss and recommend operating improvement.

6. Method: Installed by management and consultant.

7. Design: Before-and-after measures of experimental case only.

8. Productivity Results: Over one-and-a-half-year period, delays in the processing of orders decreased from about 25% to 1%.

9. Other Results: None reported.

10. Intervening Effects: None reported.

*11. Limitations: A. Absence of control group.
C. Productivity limited to delay-measure.
E. Post-strike climate; prior record of late processing.
F. Single case.

1. Reference: Karasu, T.B., Stein, S.P. & Charles, E.S. A preliminary
   study of the elimination of the internship: A comparative study of
   performance of internship- and non-internship-trained residents in a
   psychiatric inpatient setting. Archives of General Psychiatry, 1974,
   31, 269-272.

2. Conclusions: Psychiatric residents whose training excluded an internship receive lower ratings and give evidence of lower-quality patient
   care than those whose training included an internship; patients of the
   latter appear to have longer hospitalization.*

3. Organization: Bronx Municipal Hospital Center psychiatric service,
   94 beds in four wards staffed by psychiatric-residency program of
   Albert Einstein College of Medicine, Jacobi Hospital.

4. Workers: 28 psychiatric residents, 14 in experimental and 14 in control group.

5. Program: Internship was omitted from training of experimental group
   but retained in training of control group.

6. Method: Installed by management.

7. Design: Post-training comparison of experimental and control groups.

8. Productivity Results: For control group, average length of stay of
   eight patients was four days longer (statistically significant);
   quality of records and of note reports was better in certain respects;
   ratings by ward personnel were statistically higher in four out of
   five categories.

9. Other Results: None reported.

10. Intervening Effects: None reported.

*11. Limitations: C. Ratings.
                   E. Small and possibly unrepresentative sample.

DOT: 183,529   #47
SIC: D-204
Program: 14
Criterion: 1,3,5,6,9,15

1. Reference: Ketchum, L.D. Paper presented at the American Association
   for the Advancement of Science symposium "Humanizing of Work," Philadelphia, Pennsylvania, December 1972. Cited in E.M. Glaser, <u>Improving
   the quality of worklife ... And in the process, improving productivity.</u>
   Los Angeles: Human Interaction Research Institute, 1974, pp. 57-69.
   (For an earlier report of this project, see Abstract No. 99.)

2. Conclusions: Changing to team-centered production improved numerous
   indices of productivity.*

3. Organization: Gaines Pet Food Plant (Post Division of General Foods),
   Topeka, Kansas.

4. Workers: Plant team- leaders and members.

5. Program: Selection of 6 managers as team leaders, with subsequent
   interpersonal-skill development. Selection of 63 production workers.
   Production centered around team units which were formed for processing,
   packing/shipping, and office duties; these functions were rotated
   within teams; two teams handled quality control. Eleven employees
   comprised safety committee.

6. Method: Installed by management and consultants.

7. Design: Before-and-after measures of experimental and of non-equivalent
   comparison group (industry as whole).

8. Productivity Results: Productivity increased within a range of 10-40%
   per man-day. Company absenteeism rate of .05% compared with industry
   rate of 10%. Over nine months, turnover was negligible, as were theft
   and misuse of property. 4.4 injuries/illnesses per 100 full-time employees compared with industry rate of 19.3.
   (Glaser reports March 1974 update of results by E.R. Dulworth: cost
   savings 20-40% greater than other plants (about $2 million per year
   in savings); about 80% less rejects than normal business rate; absenteeism rate of about 1%; turnover about 10%, compared with 15% parent-
   company rate.)

9. Other Results: Management reported improved job-satisfaction and
   discernible improvement in employee morale and in work climate.

10. Intervening Effects: None reported.

*11. Limitations: B. Non-equivalence of comparison groups.
                    F. No tests of significance.

DOT: 63,381   #48
SIC: I-481
Program: 4,6
Criterion: 2,3,6,9,15

1. Reference: Kim, J.S. & Hamner, W.C. Effect of performance feedback and
   goal setting on productivity and satisfaction in an organizational
   setting. Journal of Applied Psychology, 1976, 61, 48-57.

2. Conclusions: Goal setting improved service ratings, cost performance,
   and safety. The addition of formal feedback, regardless of whether it
   was provided by the supervisor or self-determined, further improved some
   but not all results.*

3. Organization: Four plants in a large Midwestern telephone company within the Bell system.

4. Workers: 113 blue-collar, unionized employees. Approximately 60% were
   between the ages of 40 and 60; 40% were women. Their jobs included:
   building-equipment mechanic, motor mechanic, building-services worker,
   cleaner, and stocker. Six work groups were studied in each of three
   plants and seven in the fourth plant. Each group was composed of from
   three to eight employees.

5. Program: Goal setting plus different kinds of feedback: (a) Extrinsic
   feedback only: Each Monday, groups received feedback from foreman on
   how many workers had met weekly goals; at same time, goals for current
   week were set; during week, foreman praised employees' performance when
   they exceeded past week's or company's goals; meetings were short, informal, without adverse feedback. (b) Intrinsic feedback only: Monday
   meetings with foreman to set goals; on Friday, workers rated themselves
   on number of days absent, safety, amount of money spent/budgeted, sub-
   jective service quality; were trained (by supervisor) to use rating
   form; kept forms until, after 90 days, turned in an anonymous summary.
   (c) Extrinsic and intrinsic feedback: Monday meetings with foreman; on
   Friday, employees turned in ratings, which foreman used on the following Monday for group feedback and for goal setting; during week, praise
   for exceeding goals. (d) Goal setting alone: Each Monday, instructions
   given, with no specific formal feedback, although might receive informal
   feedback.

6. Method: Installed by management.

7. Design: Non-equivalent comparison groups consisting of four experimental groups. Group 1 (N = 37) received extrinsic feedback; Group 2
   (N = 26) received intrinsic feedback; Group 3 (N = 26) received both extrinsic and intrinsic feedback; Group 4 (N = 24) received goal setting
   (informal feedback) alone. Compared pre-experimental performance and
   subsequent measurements among the four groups after 30, 60 and 90 days.

8. Productivity Results: All four conditions resulted in improved cost-
   performance; better with the three formal-feedback groups than with

103

the informal-feedback group; among the three formal-feedback groups, there were no significant differences in cost performance. All programs improved safety performance, with the formal-feedback conditions some- what (but not significantly) superior to informal-feedback. In all groups, supervisors' service ratings improved significantly with ratings in the goal-setting-alone group significantly higher than in the three formal-feedback groups combined; the greatest improvement in service- performance was in the extrinsic-feedback group. The absenteeism rate (which was initially low) was not affected over time or among feedback conditions.

9. Other Results: Among conditions, no significant differences were found in satisfaction, as measured by the Job Descriptive Index. Over time, significant increase on two aspects (promotion and supervision), and significant decrease on one (pay).

10. Intervening Effects: None reported.

*11. Limitations: B. Non-equivalence of comparison groups.
                    C. Limited time period of measuring results.

1. Reference: Kimberly, J.R. & Nielsen, W.R. Organization development
   and change in organizational performance. Administrative Science
   Quarterly, 1975, 20, 191-206.

2. Conclusions: An extensive organizational development program was
   followed by better quantity, quality, and profitability of plant
   performance, apparently mediated by improved organizational climate
   and supervisory behavior.*

3. Organization: Large multiplant, multidivisional corporation's auto-
   motive division, with about 2,600 hourly and 200 salaried employees.

4. Workers: Five hierarchical levels of hourly employees, foremen,
   general foremen, assistant superintendents, and superintendents,
   with plant manager overseeing total plant operation.

5. Program: Six phases of Organization Development (OD) program (from
   December 1969 through March 1971): (a) Initial diagnosis, with
   interviews and group meetings. (b) Team-skills training, with 25-men
   group-exercises during 2½-day workshop of foremen and superintendents.
   (c) Data confrontation, with work-groups reviewing data, determining
   problems, and making preliminary recommendations. (d) Action planning,
   with specific recommendations. (e) Team building, with natural work-
   group meeting for two days to identify blocks to effectiveness and to
   develop changed goals and plans. (f) Intergroup building, with two-
   day meetings of plant's interdependent groups to establish cooperation,
   clarify shared goals and problems.

6. Method: Installed by management and consultants.

7. Design: Before-, during-, and after-comparisons of experimental group
   only, with time-series measures of organizational climate and supervisory-behavior perceptions just before and after program,--and of
   organizational performance on daily basis for 15 months before, 14
   months during, and 12 months after program.

8. Productivity Results: (a) Rate of production: declined for before-
   and-during-OD comparison, and recovery after OD; no significant difference before vs. after OD. (b) Production-index variance: significant
   improvement for before-and-after-OD comparison. (c) Quality level:
   significant decline for before-and-during-OD comparison; significant
   increase after OD, with significant before-and-after-OD comparison.
   (d) Quality variance: improvement after OD. (e) Average-monthly-profit
   index: decline during and increase after OD, with significant improvements shown in comparisons during-and-after- and before-and-after-OD.

9. Other Results: None reported.

10. Intervening Effects: First-line supervisors were perceived to be improved on all supervisory-behavior items. Participants perceived more favorable organizational climate, including trust, support, open communications, and autonomy.

*11. Limitations: A. Absence of control group.

DOT: 689
SIC: D-399
Program: 8
Criterion: 1,6

1. Reference: King, A.S. Expectation effects in organizational change. <u>Administrative Science Quarterly</u>, 1974, <u>19</u>, 221-230.

2. Conclusions: In influencing productivity, the type of job change introduced may not be as important as the type of expectation held by personnel, although neither may influence absenteeism.*

3. Organization: Four Midwestern plants of a clothing-pattern manufacturer.

4. Workers: Each plant had 10 six-man machine crews (total N = 240) and 30 managerial personnel (total N = 120). For all crew members, tenure surpassed three months; all had favorable prior attendance and performance-evaluations.

5. Program: Two types of job change were introduced, along with two types of managerial expectation. Four different combinations of job change and expectation were made, comprising the four experimental treatments, each treatment in one of the four plants. The job changes were (a) Job enlargement: jobs included setup and inspection in addition to machine folding. (b) Job rotation: switching among three tasks at scheduled intervals. The expectations were established by telling managers either that (1) the job changes would increase output or that (2) they would not change output, but would improve industrial relations.

6. Method: Installed by management.

7. Design: For comparison groups, multiple time-series measures taken monthly for 12-month pre- and post-experimental periods.

8. Productivity Results: Following the intervention, average daily output per machine crew was significantly higher for the plants with managers told to expect increased output than for the plants with managers told to expect improved relations. No difference was found between the plants undergoing job enlargement vs. rotation. No difference in mandays lost through job absence was found for either the expectation or job-change comparisons.

9. Other Results: None reported.

10. Intervening Effects: Workers and managers had stronger expectations that job enrichment would improve output than in those with managers told to expect improved relations. Managers told to expect improved relations, however, exhibited significantly lower expectations concerning those relations than did managers told to expect improved output; no difference was found at the worker level.

*11. Limitations: B. Possible non-equivalence of comparison groups.
                   F. Statistical data failed to make clear which specific
                      expectation treatment led to greater before-after
                      changes.

DOT: 24
SIC: H-602
Program: 8
Criterion: 1,2,3,5

1. Reference: Kraft, W.R., Jr. & Williams, K.L. Job redesign improves productivity. Personnel Journal, 1975, 54, 393-397.

2. Conclusions: Job redesign coupled with supervisory training may improve performance and turnover.*

3. Organization: Bankers Trust Co., New York.

4. Workers: Three clerical sections of Deposit Accounting Division; described as having initial low productivity, high error rate, unacceptable turnover.

5. Program: Supervisors were given three-day course in motivational theory. Redesign of jobs included task combination, vertical loading (additional responsibility), development of clerical appraisals system, increased self-evaluation, increased contact with client.

6. Method: Installed by management and consultants.

7. Design: Before-and-after comparisons of experimental group only.

8. Productivity Results: Regular and Special Accounts Division: forgeries paid decreased 56%; misfiled items decreased 19.2%; complaints from other departments decreased 20-30% per month; staff level in file and referral areas was reduced 16%; turnover declined from 38 to 14; total cost per standard hour decreased from $7.62 to $6.61. Business Accounts Division: decrease in error rate from 2.46% to 1.40% in three-month period, with decrease in total-cycle error rate from .65% to .53%; 22% savings in staff level; productivity index increased from 88.3% to 108.6%; turnover declined from 15 to 7; unit cost fell from $9.83 to $8.90. Accounting Control Division: over three months, 34.7% improvement in setup clerical capacity; 30 productive hours per month were added; unit cost fell from $7.13 to $3.24.

9. Other Results: None reported.

10. Intervening Effects: Regular and Special Accounts Division: survey of supervisory time apportioned showed an increase from 17% to 68% in time available for subordinate development.

*11. Limitations: A. Absence of control group.
                    E. Initially, high turnover, high error rate, low productivity.
                    F. No tests of significance.

DOT: 7-unspecified, 26-28   #52
SIC: D-unspecified
Program: 1
Criterion: 2,4,15

1. Reference: Kraut, A.I. The entrance of black employees into traditionally white jobs. _Academy of Management Journal_, 1975, 18, 610-615.

2. Conclusions: Following affirmative action in a manufacturing company,
   no differences were found between matched black and white employees in
   average job-performance ratings and in progress.

3. Organization: Large manufacturing company.

4. Workers: Seven black salesmen and eight black repairmen randomly
   chosen from those who completed initial training, but were with the
   company less than two years; matched with 15 white employees.

5. Program: Firm joined United States government's Plans for Progress
   program: minority group members were placed on previously "white" jobs.

6. Method: Installed by management.

7. Design: Comparison of two groups, after the program was installed, by
   interviewing worker pairs and their managers.

8. Productivity Results: No significant difference was found between the
   performance ratings of the two groups. Follow-up three years later
   again failed to find a significant difference. The two groups exhibited similar promotion rates and promotability status.

9. Other Results: 90% of blacks reported friendly co-worker and customer
   reception. Significantly more blacks reported relationships as better
   than expected.

10. Intervening Effects: As reported by managers, significantly more
    special assistance was initially given to blacks than to whites.

11. Limitations: C. Knowledge of program may have affected results.
                  E. Possibly unrepresentative sample.
                  F. Small sample.

1. Reference: LaCapra, L. Trying out the four day work week. <u>Public Personnel Management</u>, 1973, <u>2</u>, 216-220.

2. Conclusions: Adoption of a 4/40 work schedule did not create observable lasting effects over a 10-week trial period.*

3. Organization: Port Authority of New York and New Jersey.

4. Workers: White-collar employees in two departments.

5. Program: Conversion from 5-day, 40-hour workweek to 4-day, 40-hour workweek.

6. Method: Installed by management.

7. Design: Measures taken during ten-week trial period and compared to measures for prior similar periods; experimental groups only.

8. Productivity Results: During experimental period, no significant differences in workload statistics occurred in either direction.

9. Other Results: 31% of the supervisors indicated that the unit as a whole experienced difficulty maintaining its previous output level; 14% of the supervisors felt that productivity had improved. Morale was said to be good initially, but this decreased as the experiment progressed.

10. Intervening Effects: None reported.

*11. Limitations: A. Absence of control groups.
                    D. Program peculiarities (limited duration of experiment).

1. Reference: Latham, G.P. & Bales, J.J. The "practical significance" of Locke's theory of goal setting. <u>Journal of Applied Psychology</u>, 1975, <u>60</u>, 122-124.

2. Conclusions: The specification of clear and difficult (but attainable) production goals may lead to improved productivity.*

3. Organization: Oklahoma timber-logging operations.

4. Workers: Six crews, each consisting of 6 to 10 workers, including a truck driver. Each crew fells trees, loads them, and trucks them to a mill. Workers are hourly-paid and unionized.

5. Program: The drivers in charge of each crew were responsible for efficient loading. The production goals were traditionally defined in terms of "doing their best." The new program entailed the stipulation of the difficult but attainable goal of 94% of allowable net weight.

6. Method: Installed by timberlands management and union leadership.

7. Design: Time-series measures taken for three months (July-September) prior to program and for nine months (October-June) after; experimental group only.

8. Productivity Results: Prompt and substantial increase in productivity.

9. Other Results: None reported.

10. Intervening Effects: None reported.

*11. Limitations: A. Absence of control group.
                   C. Special nature of productivity measure.
                   E. Small firms; simple, clear operations.
                   F. Small sample.
                      No tests of significance.

1. Reference: Latham, G.P. & Kinne, S.B., III. Improving job performance through training in goal setting. Journal of Applied Psychology, 1974, 59, 187-191.

2. Conclusions: The specification of clear and difficult (but attainable) production goals, along with the provision of information on perform- ance, led to improved productivity. Absenteeism also improved, but not turnover or injury rates.*

3. Organization: A pulpwood-production company.

4. Workers: Training and control groups, each composed of 10 logging crews. Crews were matched on crew size, production systems, geographic location, and presence of this characteristic: previously, no produc- tion goal had been set.

5. Program: Three-month experimental period of giving to experimental crews production goals for each day and/or week, along with tally meters to self-monitor and evaluate performance.

6. Method: Installed by company foresters.

7. Design: Throughout experimental period, weekly measures taken in ex- perimental and control groups following change in former.

8. Productivity Results: The production of the experimental crews was significantly higher than that of the control group. Absenteeism was significantly higher in the control group. No significant differences were shown for individual sawhands' production, and for turnover and injury rates.

9. Other Results: None reported.

10. Intervening Effects: None reported.

*11. Limitations: C. Short duration of observations.
E. Relatively simple, clear operations.

1. Reference: Latham, G.P. & Yukl, G.A. Assigned versus participative
   goal setting with educated and uneducated woods workers. *Journal of
   Applied Psychology*, 1975, 60, 299-302.

2. Conclusions: The favorable productivity effects of goal setting,
   especially when done with worker participation, may be greater for
   marginal, low-education, black workers than for more educated, white
   ones.*

3. Organization: Logging company; various Southern locations.

4. Workers: First sample: 24 educationally disadvantaged, independent
   logging crews; primarily from North Carolina; marginal workers described as having unsatisfactory productivity/turnover/absenteeism; most
   were black. Second sample: 24 educated crews; primarily from Okla-
   homa/Arkansas region; all were white; mean education 12.9 years. Both
   samples were matched on previous production; no prior goal set.

5. Program: Three goal-setting conditions: (a) "Do your best" for comparison. (b) Participative goal-setting, with men setting specific
   weekly production goals. (c) Assigned goal-setting, with managers
   setting specific, hard goals--without consulting the crews.

6. Method: Installed by management and consultants.

7. Design: Random assignment of crews to one of the above goal-setting
   conditions; time-series measures taken weekly for eight weeks.

8. Productivity Results: First sample: mean performance significantly
   different across three conditions: lowest in "do your best" and highest
   in participative goal-setting condition; goal difficulty was set significantly higher in participative than in assigned goal-setting condition; goals were attained significantly more often in participative than
   in assigned goal-setting condition. Second sample: no significant
   differences in mean performance across conditions; in goal difficulty;
   or in goal attainment.

9. Other Results: None reported.

10. Intervening Effects: None reported.

*11. Limitations: C. Short duration of observations.
                   E. Relatively simple, clear operations.
                      Little involvement (counseling, encouragement) by
                      managers in educated sample.

1. Reference: Latham, G.P. & Yukl, G.A. Effects of assigned and participative goal setting on performance and job satisfaction. Journal of
Applied Psychology, 1976, 61, 166-171.

2. Conclusions: After ten weeks, programs involving either assigned goals
or participative goal setting were followed by significant improvement
in productivity. Interestingly, however, job satisfaction declined,
indicating that productivity increases may not have been due to positive
motivation.

3. Organization: Large corporate setting with ten word-processing centers,
three to six typists in each center.

4. Workers: A total of 45 female typists, 20 randomly assigned to the
participative goal-setting condition, and 21 to the assigned-goal condition; 4 typists in the comparison group.

5. Program: (a) Assigned-goal condition: each typist was given by her
supervisor, a difficult but attainable weekly production-goal; the goal
was based on the previous week's performance, which was also fed back
during goal assignment. (b) Participative goal-setting condition:
weekly goals were set by the typists and their supervisor. (c) Comparison group: no specified goals.

6. Method: Installed by management and consultants.

7. Design: Measurements taken six weeks before the experiment and five and
ten weeks after its installation, and compared for different conditions.

8. Productivity Results: On comparing output before the goal-setting program and ten weeks after (but not five weeks after), significant improvement was shown both in the assigned and in the participative group.
There was no significant difference between the goal-setting groups in
goal attainment, level of goal difficulty, or productivity.

9. Other Results: After the program was compared to a pretest, job satisfaction declined significantly in the two goal-setting groups. None of
the following six worker-characteristics affected the results: education, time in present job, self-esteem, internal/external control, need
for independence, need for achievement.

10. Intervening Effects: The influence scores reported by the typists were
significantly higher in the participative than in the assigned program,
indicating the irrelevance of perceived influence in explaining the
similarity of the two outcomes.

11. Limitations: A. Control group not used in statistical comparison.
C. Short duration of observations.

DOT: 7-unspecified,80   #58
SIC: D-unspecified,D-371
Program: 11
Criterion: 1,2,3,12

1. Reference: Likert, R. Improving cost performance with cross-functional teams. <u>Conference Board Record</u>, 1975, <u>12</u>(9), 51-59.

2. Conclusions: The formation of teams consisting of workers from different functions may improve productivity.*

3. Organization: An auto assembly plant; an assembly plant of another manufacturing company.

4. Workers: In auto plant, about 200 workers making cushions for automobiles. In other company, seven working-floor teams with 30-300 members in each team; functions including shipping, construction and maintenance, operations of continuous-process units.

5. Program: Cross-functional teams containing persons from different functions--to link the organization horizontally. Teams are responsible for the complete task--setting production, cost and quality goals; setting delivery dates; deciding how work is organized; designing jobs. Each team has a supervisor or someone with overall responsibility who links the team to other, related teams and who supervises subordinates in his vertical, functional line.

6. Method: Installed by management and consultants.

7. Design: Before-and-after measures of experimental groups only.

8. Productivity Results: Auto plant: 28% improvement in productivity; scrap cost declined. Other company: 20% increase in production, with only a 10% increase in costs; in one area, minor maintenance costs decreased by 40%; insignificant number of grievances.

9. Other Results: None reported.

10. Intervening Effects: None reported.

*11. Limitations: A. Absence of control group.
                  F. No tests of significance.

DOT: 185,290   #59
SIC: G-54
Program: 3,10,11
Criterion: 1,3

1. Reference: Luke, R., Block, P., Davey, J. & Averch, V. A structural approach to organizational change. <u>Journal of Applied Behavioral Science</u>, 1973, <u>9</u>, 611-635.

2. Conclusions: Changing an authority structure from one of close supervision to one providing employees with more participation as well as with training appeared to improve organizational performance.*

3. Organization: Large retail food chain.

4. Workers: Middle- and top-management executives.

5. Program: Change from a system of close supervision of employees to one with emphasis on encouraging consultation by employees. In addition, employees were given training. Structural alteration of management effected by redesigning the chain of command, creating new roles, changing existing roles, and modifying the managerial style of middle and top management.

6. Method: Installed by management.

7. Design: Experimental district of 15 stores compared with five other districts on various performance-measures.

8. Productivity Results: For initial quarter of the study, the experimental district had the smallest decrease in sales and the smallest increase in labor ratio--and was one of the two that showed an increase in sales per man-hour. At the end of the first year, the experimental district rose to the top and had outperformed the five comparison districts.

9. Other Results: Opposition to the relinquishing of line authority decreased and supervisors exhibited more positive attitudes toward the new structure.

10. Intervening Effects: None reported.

*11. Limitations: D. Possible non-equivalence of comparison group. Small number of cases.
E. Structure may be especially relevant to decentralized retail operations. Introduction of training as well as of participation.
F. No tests of significance.

117

1. Reference: Maher, J.R. & Overbaugh, W.B. Better inspection performance through job enrichment. In J.R. Maher (ed.), New perspectives in job enrichment. New York: Van Nostrand, Reinhold, 1971, pp. 79-89.

2. Conclusions: A job-enrichment program seems to have increased output and morale of workers, with signs of partial decline after a year.*

3. Organization: Large electronics manufacturing plant.

4. Workers: 70 workers who inspected parts manufactured in the plant and by suppliers.

5. Program: A job-enrichment program for inspectors, which attempted to increase job challenge and feelings of responsibility. The program consisted of abolishing step-by-step quality-inspection and installing a final-inspection department. A Machining Quality Assurance department was also created, where many former inspectors were promoted to the enriched job of Machining Quality Analyst. Similar job changes were made in the Supplier Quality Assurance area.

6. Method: Installed by management.

7. Design: Before-and-after measures of experimental groups only. Measures covered results one year later, and period of approximately five years.

8. Productivity Results: The first year, results of the program included:
   (a) The acceptance rate of purchased parts improved from 92.2% to 97.5%.
   (b) Time required for inspection of purchased parts decreased from 1.5 hours per job to .7 hours per job. (c) 50% decrease in inspection-time. (d) 50% decrease in defective-quality lots found in assembly. Beyond one year, there was some decline in performance of inspectors, but not of quality analysts.

9. Other Results: Morale is said to have increased. After a year, morale declined somewhat for inspectors, but not for quality analysts.

10. Intervening Effects: None reported.

*11. Limitations: A. Absence of control groups.
                    C. Impressionistic evaluation of morale.
                    F. No tests of significance.

1. Reference: Malone, E.L. The Non-Linear Systems experiment in participative management. _Journal of Business_, 1975, 48, 52-64.

2. Conclusions: Because of various factors including ambiguity of new
   organizational plan, marketing problems besetting the industry, etc.,
   the installation of a system featuring participative management was not
   followed by anticipated benefits.*

3. Organization: Non-Linear Systems, Inc., of Del Mar, California; manufactures digital electrical measuring-instruments.

4. Workers: About 340 employees in 1960s (75% were male), and about 110
   at present.

5. Program: Participative management initiated in 1960-1961 (largely
   abandoned in 1965). Key features included: vertical organization replaced by three "zones"; assembly lines replaced by 30 department
   units/project teams, each consisting of 3 to 12 employees and department manager in one room, responsible for completed instruments,
   setting own pace, deciding on task allocation, settling own internal
   problems; on-the-job training provided for each new employee; time
   clocks eliminated; separate accounting and inspection departments
   eliminated; hourly workers put on salary.

6. Method: Installed by management and consultants.

7. Design: Before-and-after measures of experimental case only.

8. Productivity Results: Decrease in profits led to program abandonment.
   No production records reported, but appeared to be no decrease in man-
   hours required per instrument or increase in plant efficiency. Initial
   increase in sales was not commensurate with increase in sales costs;
   sales later declined. No change in turnover (about 4-5%). High turnover of department managers (from 1962 to 1965, 13 out of 30 left).
   Absenteeism rate remained stable.

9. Other Results: None reported.

10. Intervening Effects: Indications of confusion and frustration on part
    of managers.

*11. Limitations: A. Absence of control group.
                   D. Unusual zone-type of organization.
                   E. Manufacturing, assembly workers with high level of
                      education, and well trained; climate sympathetic to
                      human relations movement; increase in competition;
                      dominant president.
                   F. No tests of significance.

1. Reference: McCormick, J.H. An old standby that still works. Training and Development Journal, 1971, 26(10), 3-7.

2. Conclusions: Job Instruction Training program combined with on-the-job assignments for supervisors may produce tangible dollar-valued results in work areas.*

3. Organization: Abbott Laboratories.

4. Workers: 20 production-line supervisors from a wide variety of departments.

5. Program: A 25-hour Job Instruction Training program presented over ten weeks. The program included classroom discussions and exercises; on-the-job assignments that focused on analysis of difficulties being experienced by each individual supervisor; and plans to remedy the particular situation by retraining subordinates.

6. Method: Installed by management.

7. Design: Productivity results are described for the various supervisors who participated; essentially, a collection of brief case-reports.

8. Productivity Results: 17 of the 20 supervisors are reported as showing tangible results of job training. For example, one participant retrained approximately 30 of her employees and succeeded in raising the average productivity of her subordinates about 14%.

9. Other Results: None reported.

10. Intervening Effects: None reported.

*11. Limitations: A. Absence of control group.
                   F. No tests of significance.

DOT: unspecified   #63
SIC: H-63
Program: 13
Criterion: 1,2,5

1. Reference: McDermott, R.F. Report to the board of directors on the results of the four-day workweek experiment. Summarized in A.S. Glickman & Z.H. Brown, Changing schedules of work: Patterns and implications. Washington, D.C.: W.E. Upjohn Institute for Employment Research, 1974, pp. 26-27.

2. Conclusions: The four-day workweek may serve to increase productivity.*

3. Organization: United States Automobile Association, an insurance company.

4. Workers: Approximately 3,000 employees in the San Antonio office of that company.

5. Program: With few exceptions, the workforce was placed on a four-day week, working nine-and-a-half hours per day with half-hour lunch period. Paid holidays were abolished, and more days of vacation were accrued.

6. Method: Installed by management.

7. Design: In experimental group only, measures before and one year after program-installation.

8. Productivity Results: The average "turn-around" time to return a policy to an applicant decreased from 10.5 days to 6.8 days. Individual production records improved. The error ratio dropped from 7.2% to 6.1%. Job turnover decreased from 25% to approximately 18%.

9. Other Results: None reported.

10. Intervening Effects: Introduction of a new computer into the process may have increased efficiency of work done. 96% of workers thought program was good idea, 94% liked job better, 93% thought longer day was not too fatiguing.

*11. Limitations: A. Absence of control group.
                  D. Introduction of computerization as well as of schedule change.
                  F. No tests of significance.

1. Reference: NcNulty, L.A. Job enrichment: How to make it work.
   Supervisory Management, 1973, 18(9), 7-15.

2. Conclusions: Job enrichment seems to have been followed by quality and
   cost improvements.*

3. Organization: Chase Manhattan Bank.

4. Workers: Money-transfer division--typists, checkers, and signers.

5. Program: Job enrichment: included lateral and vertical job-loading
   (more tasks, more responsibility); teamwork units; customer identification and feedback. Signers were given more responsibilities (of
   checkers) and were grouped with typists, in one room.

6. Method: Installed by management.

7. Design: Before-and-after measures of experimental group only.

8. Productivity Results: Error rates decreased 13%. Checkers were no
   longer required; this generated cost savings.

9. Other Results: None reported.

10. Intervening Effects: None reported.

*11. Limitations: A. Absence of control group.
                    F. No tests of significance.

1. Reference: Mehr, J. Evaluating nontraditional training for psychiatric aides. Hospital and Community Psychiatry, 1971, 22, 315-318.

2. Conclusions: An intensive training-program for experienced psychiatric aides can improve knowledge and job performance.

3. Organization: Elgin State Hospital, Illinois.

4. Workers: Experimental group = 71 psychiatric aides; length of employment ranged from 2 to 21 years. 15 males, 56 females; ages ranged from 22 to 72 years. Comparison group = 30 aides.

5. Program: 220-hour training-program for promotion of psychiatric aides to the next higher level in the state civil-service classification. Program included lectures, discussions by small groups, role playing, encounter groups, and practice in remotivation techniques.

6. Method: Installed by hospital management.

7. Design: Before-and-after measures of experimental group compared with non-equivalent comparison group. For 33 randomly selected trainees, retest measurement followed six months later.

8. Productivity Results: Following training for experimental group, trainees' performance ratings by supervisors improved significantly in seven areas related to material taught in the course. No significant changes found for comparison group.

9. Other Results: The experimental group scored significantly better on the post-training test of course-related material. Retesting of 33 aides six months after training showed retention of course-material by trainees.

10. Intervening Effects: None reported.

11. Limitations: B. Non-equivalence of comparison group.
                  C. Performance evaluated by supervisory ratings.

1. Reference: Mikesell, J.L., Wilson, J.A. & Lawther, W. Training program and evaluation model. Public Personnel Management, 1975, 4, 405-411.

2. Conclusions: Training in substantive information may lead to improved performance quality and reduced costs.*

3. Organization: Indiana Department of Revenue.

4. Workers: 39 tax auditors.

5. Program: Tax-audit workshop divided into three segments: case situations simulating communication- and taxpayer-relations problems; step-by-step audit guides; and final audit of a simulated corporation.

6. Method: Installed by management and Indiana University.

7. Design: Before-and-after measures of two trained groups and of non-equivalent control group (Audit Division as a whole).

8. Productivity Results: Trainees showed greater improvement than comparison group in rate of taxpayer-errors found, and in amount of new revenue generated. Corrections and supplemental required audits per auditor fell 44% for Group 1 and 34% for Group 2. No-change audits also declined in both groups (20% and 8%).

9. Other Results: None reported.

10. Intervening Effects: Chart describes trainees' evaluations of extent to which the three workshop-segments succeeded in meeting their needs.

*11. Limitations: B. Non-equivalence of comparison group.
                   F. No tests of significance.

1. Reference: Miller, L.A., Roberts, R.R., et al. Studies in continuing
   education for rehabilitation counselors (SRS 12-55239-70). Iowa: University of Iowa, October 1971. (NTIS No. PB-215 634.)

2. Conclusions: Following a program designed to give instruction and
   feedback, no change was found in quality of counselor-performance.*

3. Organization: Iowa State Division of Rehabilitation Education and
   Services.

4. Workers: 96 counselors employed in 17 field offices.

5. Program: Four-month continuing-education program in skill development,
   also, during monthly conferences, providing each counselor with two
   sources of feedback (client reports and supervisory critiques) concerning his interview skills.

6. Method: Installed by management and University of Iowa.

7. Design: Before-and-after measures of experimental group only.

8. Productivity Results: Over the experimental period, there was no
   change in client evaluations of counselor service.

9. Other Results: None reported.

10. Intervening Effects: Counselors' reactions showed that less than half
    used instructional manual or had critique conferences with supervisors.

*11. Limitations: A. Absence of control group.
                   C. Limited to ratings.
                   D. Lack of supervisor participation; little time given or
                      interest shown by counselors.
                   F. No tests of significance.

DOT: unspecified
SIC: D-28
Program: 13
Criterion: 6,15

1. Reference: Nord, W.R. & Costigan, R.   Worker adjustment to the four-day week; A longitudinal study. <u>Journal of Applied Psychology</u>, 1973, <u>58</u>, 60-66.

2. Conclusions: Absenteeism may decrease as a result of conversion to a nine-and-a-half-hour day, four-day workweek. Unfavorable effects on home life and on attitudes may appear over time.*

3. Organization: St. Louis-based, medium-sized, non-unionized pharmaceutical company.

4. Workers: Foremen, group leaders, and lower-level employees, who were employed at the plant for at least 10 of the 12 months covered by the survey. Average age of the employees was in the late forties.

5. Program: Conversion from eight-hour day, five-day workweek to nine-and-a-half-hour day, four-day workweek.

6. Method: Installed by management.

7. Design: In experimental company only, measures taken 6 weeks, 13 weeks and 1 year after the initial trial period.

8. Productivity Results: Absenteeism decreased significantly.

9. Other Results: Workers perceived more job changes over time. Initially, there were positive attitudes toward the four-day workweek, with some later decline. There was a decrease in the number of hours of sleep; negative effects on home life were reported in later surveys.

10. Intervening Effects: None reported.

*11. Limitations: A. Absence of control group.
                   C. Measures confounded with seasonal variations.

1. Reference: Oetting, E.R. & Miller, C.D. Job coaching: The effect on work adjustment of the disadvantaged (DLMA 82-06-70-19-1). Colorado: Colorado State University, January 1973. (NTIS No. PB-221 440.)

2. Conclusions: Job coaching did not affect the job tenure of disadvantaged clients.*

3. Organization: Colorado State University Experimental Laboratory, four manpower agencies, and firms into which clients were placed.

4. Workers: Disadvantaged persons referred by Denver-area manpower agencies, or by friends. Sample included blacks, chicanos, and anglos (N = 199).

5. Program: Intensive job-coaching by paraprofessionals, who actively scheduled meetings; followed workers into community over a considerable period of time; and extended contact to placement and other services.

6. Method: Installed by University faculty and U.S. Department of Labor.

7. Design: Randomly matched samples in experimental and control groups.

8. Productivity Results: Job coaching had no effect on the workers' ability to hold jobs after placement, compared to controls.

9. Other Results: Job coaching had no effect on percent presently working or on percent fired. Coached workers obtained significantly more jobs, and their average weekly pay was significantly lower.

10. Intervening Effects: None reported.

*11. Limitations: D. Limited access to scattered jobs, to employers, and to supervisors resulted in the following: coaches were not able to establish satisfactory relationships with supervisors; did not receive job-performance feedback; and were not able to negotiate after client had failed on job.

1. Reference: Paul, G.L., McInnis, T.L. & Mariotto, M.J. Objective performance outcomes associated with two approaches to training mental
   health technicians in milieu and social learning programs. Journal of
   Abnormal Psychology, 1973, 82, 523-532.

2. Conclusions: The integration of concrete job-related behavior into
   technician training appears to be superior to academic instruction
   alone.*

3. Organization: State mental hospital.

4. Workers: Non-professional trainees. N = 14 in each of two experimental
   groups. Employees were selected from the unemployed ranks; were of
   lower-to-middle socioeconomic status. 83% were female; 16% were black;
   50% were married; 50% had children; and 17% had a minimal amount of
   prior experience with institutionalized patients. Mean age = 25.5
   years; mean educational level = 12.5 years.

5. Program: In each of two ongoing experimental patient-treatment programs, installed two methods of training non-professional mental-health
   technicians. One program was a "milieu" patient-treatment program, and
   another was a "social learning" patient-treatment program. The
   "sequential/professional" training method involved only academic instruction. The "integrated/technical" method consisted of abbreviated
   instruction integrated with clinical observation. For both experimental groups, the training method used was followed by on-the-job
   training.

6. Method: Installed by the Project Director and the Program Director.

7. Design: Measures for experimental groups only--taken after completion
   of six weeks of on-the-job training, and again six weeks after trainees
   had been functioning independently.

8. Productivity Results: On both patient-treatment programs, at both time
   intervals, employees trained by the "integrated/technical" method were
   evaluated as performing significantly better than those trained by the
   "sequential/professional" method. Civil service ratings of people
   trained by the two methods did not differ.

9. Other Results: Academic instruction resulted in greater understanding
   of principles and procedures. In both groups, academic performance was
   significantly correlated with goodness of on-the-floor performance.

10. Intervening Effects: None reported.

*11. Limitations: B. Possible non-equivalence of comparison groups.
                   C. Special performance-rating. Civil service ratings may
                      not reflect performance.

1. Reference: Pedalino, E. & Gamboa, V.U. Behavior modification and
   absenteeism: Intervention in one industrial setting. Journal of
   Applied Psychology, 1974, 59, 694-698.

2. Conclusions: Attendance and tardiness can be reduced by means of inter-
   mittent financial reward delivered via a game of chance.*

3. Organization: One manufacturing-and-distribution location of a
   multiplant company.

4. Workers: Experimental group composed of assembly-line workers, in
   departments ranging from 14 to 26 workers (total = 215); four comparison
   groups numbering 30, 43, 65, and 370, doing various manual jobs. Male.
   Mean education = eleventh grade. Mean tenure = 11.5 years. Mean wage =
   $4.86 per hour.

5. Program: Behavior modification by reinforcement of desired behavior
   (attendance), using a lottery delivering to winners a $20 weekly or
   bi-weekly payoff. Experimental period consisted of a weekly payoff or
   schedule of reinforcement (six-week Phase 1) and a bi-weekly payoff or
   schedule of reinforcement (ten-week Phase 2).

6. Method: Installed by management.

7. Design: During 32-week pre-experimental period, 16-week experimental
   period, and 22-week follow-up period, multiple time-series measures for
   experimental and comparison groups.

8. Productivity Results: In experimental group, during experimental
   period, unexcused absenteeism decreased 18% (statistically significant);
   during follow-up period after discontinuation of program, absenteeism
   climbed 30% (significant). No significant differences were found
   between Phases 1 and 2. No significant changes took place in three of
   the comparison groups, with a significant increase in absenteeism for
   one group. In experimental group, during experimental period, tardiness
   decreased.

9. Other Results: None reported.

10. Intervening Effects: None reported.

*11. Limitations: B. Non-equivalence of comparison groups.
                   D. Limited duration of experiment.
                   E. Male, blue-collar.

1. Reference: Pieper, W.J., Catrow, E.J., Swezey, R.W. & Smith E.
   <u>Automated apprenticeship training: A systematized audio-visual
   approach to self-paced job training</u> (AFHRL-TR-72-20). Pennsylvania:
   Applied Science Associates, April 1973. (NTIS No. AD-764 818.)

2. Conclusions: Low-aptitude personnel can be effectively trained via a
   method emphasizing audio-visual, skills-oriented instruction and de-
   emphasizing reading and writing skills. The approach can be used with
   both low- and high-aptitude groups. Also, the program required less
   training- and administration-time.

3. Organization: Air Force Human Resources Laboratory.

4. Workers: 60 first-term enlisted airmen designated as New Mental
   Standards (NMS) airmen; most of these men did not complete high school.
   A standard high-aptitude group was also included. The total number of
   subjects in the experimental and comparison groups were 180.

5. Program: Developed and evaluated a training-course and job-test
   suitable for NMS airmen as well as for high- or average-aptitude
   trainees. Two Automated Apprenticeship Training (AAT) courses were
   developed for Air Force Security Police Law Enforcement and Security
   Specialists. The objective was to deemphasize reading and writing
   skills by using a systematized, audio-visual approach to self-paced job-
   training, an approach designed to be compatible with on-job learning
   requirements. The format was behaviorally oriented, showing the
   trainee what to do and how to do it, and giving him time for guided
   practice.

6. Method: Installed as part of "Project 100,000," which was designed to
   accept into the military services and to train 100,000 men who previously would not have qualified, on aptitude grounds.

7. Design: The experimental trainees were compared with trainees in two
   standard programs. Each group was divided between high- and low-aptitude trainees. For each group, productivity was evaluated by supervisory ratings made after two months on the job.

8. Productivity Results: Supervisors' ratings did not differ among the
   three training programs, or between the two aptitude groups.

9. Other Results: Examination scores in the experimental program were no
   worse, and sometimes were better, than in the comparison programs. The
   experimental program produced a 30% reduction in training time, and reduced instructors' man-hour requirements 70%.

10. Intervening Effects: None reported.

11. Limitations: B. Non-equivalence of comparison groups.
                    C. Criterion limited to supervisory ratings after two months.
                    E. Study limited to special military jobs.

1. Reference: Pierce, C. & Risley, T. Improving job performance of Neighborhood Youth Corps aides in an urban recreation program. <u>Journal of Applied Behavior Analysis</u>, 1974, <u>7</u>, 207-215.

2. Conclusions: The amount of work completed is greater under a piece-rate than under an hourly-rate pay system.*

3. Organization: Employees hired by Neighborhood Youth Corps (a federal training program) and placed at Turner House (a recreation center in Kansas City).

4. Workers: Seven black adolescents; four male, three female.

5. Program: Piece vs. hourly pay. Phase 1: Before Day 1, job descriptions were drawn up; trainees received descriptions and chose jobs they wanted to do. Phase 2: After Day 5, Director threatened to fire unsatisfactory workers. Phase 3: Days 12-18, aides' pay based on percent tasks-completed rather than on hourly rate ($1.65 per hour). Phase 4: Days 19-21, aides again received hourly pay ($1.65 per hour). Phase 5: Days 22-25, pay again based on percent tasks-completed.

6. Method: Installed by management and consultants.

7. Design: Time-series measures of performance prior to, during, and after experimental pay-plan.

8. Productivity Results: Phase 1 (hourly pay): In general, employees completed 50-75% of tasks (one employee completed 90%). Phase 2 (threat): For three days, six employees increased percent tasks-completed, but then two decreased to former level; one still completed 90%. Phase 3 (piece-rate): All seven completed nearly 100%. Phase 4 (hourly pay): Over three days, average completed 35%. Phase 5 (piece-rate): Increased percent-completed again.

9. Other Results: None reported.

10. Intervening Effects: None reported.

*11. Limitations: D. Short-term duration of program.
                   E. Black adolescents.
                   F. Small sample.
                   No tests of significance.

1. Reference: Pomerleau, O.F., Bobrove, P.H. & Smith, R.H. Rewarding
   psychiatric aides for the behavioral improvement of assigned patients.
   Journal of Applied Behavioral Analysis, 1973, 6, 383-390.

2. Conclusions: Case awards, feedback, and direct supervision of psychiatric aides seem to be useful in improving behavior of patients.*

3. Organization: Psychiatric ward at Philadelphia State Hospital.

4. Workers: Psychiatric aides. N = 12; mean salary = $5,500/year; median
   age = 29 years; median education = 12 years.

5. Program: Investigated effects of supervision and of cash awards based
   upon behavioral improvement of assigned patients.

6. Method: Installed by psychology staff.

7. Design: Three overlapping phases: Phase 1 dealt with effects of non-
   contingent awards, and information about patients; Phase 2 dealt with
   effects of cash awards contingent upon improvement in patient behavior;
   Phase 3 dealt with the effects of consultation and supervision by the
   staff. Contemporary observations of patient behavior were used as
   measures of results.

8. Productivity Results: Patients behaved more appropriately when the cash
   awards to aides were increased, and behaved less appropriately when the
   awards were decreased. When not contingent on the improvement of
   patients, awards to aides produced little change in patients' behavior.
   When supervisors gave feedback to aides concerning their patients,
   patients behaved more appropriately. Direct supervision of aide-
   patient interactions was associated with an increase in appropriate
   behavior; however, "required" consultation for aides concerning their
   assigned patients was not associated.

9. Other Results: None reported.

10. Intervening Effects: None reported.

*11. Limitations: A. Absence of control group.
                   C. Rated behavioral improvement of patients was possibly
                      influenced by raters' knowledge of experiment.
                   F. Small sample.
                      No tests of significance.

1. Reference: Pommer, D.A. & Streedbeck, D. Motivating staff performance in an operant learning program for children. <u>Journal of Applied Behavior Analysis</u>, 1974, <u>7</u>, 217-222.

2. Conclusions: The public posting of job-duties--a form of goal setting--and incentive-compensation based on performance of those duties seem to increase the amount of work done.*

3. Organization: Children's Unit of the Problems-in-Living Center in Sioux Falls, South Dakota, a small residential facility for children (six) with severely maladaptive behaviors.

4. Workers: Nine house-parents of Children's Unit; household duties.

5. Program: Specification of duties and of incentive pay: (a) Public Notice (PN): Posted charts with each staff member's special duties; all staff members could read charts and know who was responsible for certain jobs. (b) Job Slip (JS): Monetary reinforcement (incentive pay); staff filled out job slip for special job or duty completed; at month's end, used as token for $1.00. Different combinations of the two procedures were implemented during 30 weeks: each alone (six-week period each), both together (two six-week periods), and baseline/neither procedure (two three-week periods).

6. Method: Installed by management and consultants.

7. Design: Time-series measures by observers of percent duties-performed were implemented over six phases.

8. Productivity Results: With PN, increase from baseline-performance (percent duties-performed) with combined PN and JS, best performance; with JS alone, decrease to level similar to average PN; with discontinuation (neither PN nor JS), decrease, but greater than original baseline; with reinstatement of PN and JS, highest level.

9. Other Results: None reported.

10. Intervening Effects: None reported.

*11. Limitations: C. Performance measured in terms of observations of duties performed.
D. Short duration of treatments.
E. House-parents; household duties.
F. No tests of significance.

1. Reference: Powell, R.M. & Schlacter, J.L. Participative management--
A panacea? Academy of Management Journal, 1971, 14, 165-173.

2. Conclusions: Increasing the levels of participation may improve
workers' job satisfaction, while productivity and absenteeism remain
unchanged or actually deteriorate.*

3. Organization: Operations Division of the Bureau of Traffic, Ohio
Department of Highways.

4. Workers: Two construction and four electrical crews responsible for
the installation of all electric utilities for the state highways
system.

5. Program: Two crews assigned to each of three levels of participation
in scheduling work. Levels of participation ranged from indirect to
representative to total responsibility.

6. Method: Installed by management.

7. Design: Before-and-after measures under each of the three experimental
conditions.

8. Productivity Results: Productivity declined in the two groups given
total responsibility, but did not change appreciably in the others.
Absenteeism became worse in five of the six groups.

9. Other Results: Job satisfaction improved under total responsibility,
but not under other conditions.

10. Intervening Effects: None reported.

*11. Limitations: A. Absence of control group.
B. Non-equivalence of comparison groups.
E. Highway crews working more or less autonomously in
the field.

1. Reference: Powers, J.E. Empirical case study for transition to more meaningful work. Paper presented at International Conference on the Quality of Working Life, Arden, New York, September 1972. Cited in E.M. Glaser, Improving the quality of worklife ... And in the process, improving productivity. Los Angeles: Human Interaction Research Institute, 1974, pp. 79-92.

2. Conclusions: Productivity improvements followed installation of a number of changes in the work system.*

3. Organization: CRYOVAC Division, W.R. Grace & Company; manufacturing facility at Camarillo, California.

4. Workers: Initial change in single department (bag-making functions). Later expanded to all major departments.

5. Program: System redesign: management committee met once a week for 20 weeks, developed new job structures (modules). Workers' pay was based on demonstrated skills-proficiency. Performance reviews were developed. Transition took place from three-on-two machine manning mode to one-on-one, with a new hierarchy of skill levels; through training, employees could progress up the ladder, with appropriate pay adjustments. Functions of quality-control inspectors were merged into line-management and operating responsibilities, and customer contact was increased.

6. Method: Installed by management.

7. Design: Before-and-after measures of experimental groups only.

8. Productivity Results: Over a two-year period, there was a 28.6% improvement in units-of-output per direct labor-dollar. Production output rose 68%, while plant personnel was reduced 9.7%. There was a 50% increase in utilization of capital equipment.

9. Other Results: None reported.

10. Intervening Effects: None reported.

*11. Limitations: A. Absence of control group.
F. No tests of significance.

1. Reference: Presley, J. & Keen, S. Better meetings lead to higher productivity: A case study. Management Review, 1975, 64(4), 16-22.

2. Conclusions: The new strategy to increase supervisor participation at weekly staff-meetings was followed by improved employee productivity.*

3. Organization: Western Regional Program Center of the Social Security Administration.

4. Workers: The experimental group was a department composed of the manager, two of her assistants and 10 supervisors, who were in charge of 180 workers. All of these received training. Five other departments served as untrained comparison groups.

5. Program: New strategy to increase supervisor participation at weekly staff meetings. The program included rearrangement of chairs; elimination of a chairperson, who was replaced by a neutral "facilitator" who kept the group focused; and introduction of a "recorder" who wrote down ideas discussed (both of these duties were rotated during the 10-week training period).

6. Method: Installed by management and consultants.

7. Design: Non-equivalent control-group design (five similar work groups).

8. Productivity Results: Six months after the program began, the experimental department's productivity profile (average number of folders cleared per gross workdays) was significantly greater than the profile of all the work groups taken together. During and after the training period, the experimental department's folder receipts and its dispatches increased, and the pending file decreased.

9. Other Results: None reported.

10. Intervening Effects: To decrease the number of pending folders, supervisors called a 15-minute meeting of the 180 employees; employees submitted 74 solutions, some of which were implemented. A significant increase in cooperative spirit and enthusiasm for meetings was observed.

*11. Limitations: B. Non-equivalence of comparison groups.

1. Reference: Quilitch, H.R. A comparison of three staff-management procedures. Journal of Applied Behavior Analysis, 1975, 8, 59-66.

2. Conclusions: The scheduling and feedback of daily activities of the
   staff of a mental health institute appears to have had favorable
   effects on their patients.*

3. Organization: Four wards in Nevada Mental Health Institute, serving 95
   mentally retarded residents.

4. Workers: Staff consisting of Chief Administrator, Assistant Chief
   Administrator, four registered nurses, two licensed practical nurses,
   17 mental health technicians, 10 "foster grandparents" (ward managers).

5. Program: Revised administrative staff-management procedures involving
   training in a variety of scheduling (goal setting) and feedback techniques over a period of several months.

6. Method: Installed by management.

7. Design: Time-series measures of residents in four wards, using Planned
   Activity Check evaluation of group care, taken·four times daily for
   total of 804 observations.

8. Productivity Results: Residents (patients) more often exhibited
   desirable behavior when staff activities were scheduled and feedback
   given to staff. Instruction alone did not appear to have much effect.

9. Other Results: None reported.

10. Intervening Effects: None reported.

*11. Limitations: A. Absence of control group.
                   B. Criterion consisted of observations and ratings of
                      patients' behavior.
                   E. Mental-health staff, retarded patients.
                   F. No tests of significance.

1. Reference: Quinn, R., Levitin, T. & Eden, D. The multimillion dollar
   misunderstanding: An attempt to reduce turnover among disadvantaged
   workers. In L. Davis & A. Chern (eds.), The quality of working life.
   New York: Free Press, 1975.

2. Conclusions: Vestibule training and orientation of workers with hard-
   core-unemployed backgrounds does not improve retention--at least when
   working conditions are basically unsatisfactory.

3. Organization: Manufacturing company described as large, multiplant,
   partially diversified and multicity.

4. Workers: 63 hard-core unemployed completed pre-employment training;
   232 men were recruited at the same time as the trainees, but did not
   receive the special training. All were black. The mean age of the
   total population was 23.4 years, and the mean educational level was
   10.4 years.

5. Program: A six-week vestibule training and orientation program was
   provided for recruits certified as hard-core unemployed. Employment
   was offered to every recruit who successfully completed the program.
   A male adviser and a female teacher staffed each class, and a job
   counselor was spread among several classes. Used standard programmed
   basic-education materials for language and mathematical skills. Goals
   included teaching a few basic skills, developing better attitudes with
   respect to achievement and self-esteem, explaining general aspects of
   employment in the company; no specific job skills were taught.

6. Method: Installed by management.

7. Design: Comparisons of turnover in trained and untrained groups over
   six-week period following job placement.

8. Productivity Results: 68% of the trained group stayed on the job at
   least six weeks; 58% of the untrained group stayed on the job for at
   least six weeks. There were no statistical differences between the
   percentages.

9. Other Results: Correlates of turnover were found to include characteristics of the worker's job, as well as the supervision he received, and
   demographic and background characteristics.

10. Intervening Effects: None reported.

11. Limitations: E. Working conditions were unpleasant and otherwise
                    unsatisfactory.

1. Reference: Randall, R. Job enrichment savings at Travelers. Management Accounting, 1973 (January), 68-69, 72.

2. Conclusions: Job enrichment seems to have increased productivity.*

3. Organization: Travelers Insurance Company of Hartford, Connecticut.

4. Workers: Entry-level keypunch operators, and clerical workers in an
accounting section.

5. Program: Job-enrichment program that restructured work into natural
units or modules.

6. Method: Installed by management.

7. Design: The study of keypunch operators involved before-and-after
comparisons of an experimental group and a control group. The study of
clerical workers in the accounting section involved only the experimental group.

8. Productivity Results: The experimental keypunch-group was reported to
have increased by nearly 40% its capacity to process work. Enrichment
of clerical jobs in the accounting section was said to have resulted in
an annual savings of $100,000, through a reduction in staff size with-
out a corresponding decrease in workload.

9. Other Results: None reported.

10. Intervening Effects: None reported.

*11. Limitations: A. Absence of control group for accounting section.
                   C. Details of measurement not provided.
                   F. No tests of significance.

DOT: 869
SIC: I-833
Program: 3
Criterion: 4

1. Reference: Roberts, M. A cost-benefit report on training disadvantaged youths for apprenticeship. <u>Training and Development Journal</u>, 1971, <u>26</u>(6), 32-35.

2. Conclusions: The entry of disadvantaged youths into building trades can be aided via a pre-apprenticeship training program. The program may have produced more employment and higher income for completers than for similar youths who were not trained. The economic pay-off from the investment in training appears to have exceeded the costs.*

3. Organization: Project Build, a pre-apprenticeship training program for disadvantaged youths.

4. Workers: 195 inner-city youths from 17½ to 24 years of age, disadvantaged by minority status, inadequate education, unemployment, and lack of work skills or experience.

5. Program: Training for placement in apprenticeships in various crafts in building trades and construction industry. The program included remedial education in mathematics and reading, as well as technical training featuring on-site work experience.

6. Method: Installed by the Greater Washington Central Labor Council in conjunction with the local building trades council.

7. Design: Compared program completers with dropouts and nonselected applicants for the year prior to application for training and for the year after training, or application for training.

8. Productivity Results: The 110 youths who completed training increased their earnings by approximately 60%, compared to about 20% for the others. Weekly earnings for completers rose roughly 55%, compared to 25%. Completers' after-tax weekly income increased by almost 60%, compared to 27%. Employment for completers increased by 10.4%, compared to 2.26%. The net benefit of pre-apprenticeship training, defined as the net increase in before-tax earnings of completers, was $1,119 one year after training.

9. Other Results: Costs per trainee and present values of pre-apprenticeship training were presented.

10. Intervening Effects: None reported.

*11. Limitations: B. Non-equivalence of comparison groups.

1. Reference: Rosen, R.A. & Rosen, H.   Orientation and job stability: The impact of supervisory and employee role-playing groups on turnover of potentially unemployed blacks.   <u>Journal of Vocational Behavior</u>, 1972, <u>2</u>, 25-37.

2. Conclusions: Orientation training of inner-city black workers and their supervisors had little or no effect on worker turnover.*

3. Organization: Public utility company located in the Midwest.

4. Workers: 170 inner-city blacks; 143 females, 27 males; average age = 20.5 years; average education = 11.5 years; more than 50% were without prior work experience; the rest had work experience of less than a year's duration.   Placed into clerical positions in service division (only females) or "helper" positions in maintenance division (both males and females).

5. Program: Supportive orientation program involving role-playing and group problem-solving in six to nine sessions over a 12-week period.

6. Method: Installed by management.

7. Design: Workers and supervisors were randomly assigned to experimental and control groups.   No significant difference was found in merit ratings between groups.

8. Productivity Results: Overall, after one year there were determined no significant differences in turnover rate that were due to differences in training.   Results were not uniform for different jobs or divisions.

9. Other Results: None reported.

10. Intervening Effects: None reported.

*11. Limitations: D. Relatively brief training.
                    E. Nature of jobs had some effect on results.

1. Reference: Rosen, H. & Turner, J. Effectiveness of two orientation
   approaches in hard core unemployed turnover and absenteeism. Journal
   of Applied Psychology, 1971, 55, 296-301.

2. Conclusions: Orientation training for the hard core unemployed was not
   followed by absenteeism rates as low as those of normal hires; but one
   of the two training programs (the one emphasizing company involvement in
   job programs) did produce turnover rates as low as those of normal
   hires. The same program also produced higher training performance-
   ratings than the other, which was focused more on personal-adjustment
   problems.*

3. Organization: Public-utility company located in the Midwest.

4. Workers: 49 black males who had not worked for at least six months
   prior to the study.

5. Program: Compared effects of a university-developed orientation
   training program vs. a company-developed training program on hard-core-
   unemployed individuals. The university training group, led by a
   psychologist trained in group psychotherapy with mixed racial groups,
   focused on discussions of job-related problems. The company program,
   although originally intended to be passive (e.g., use of lectures and
   films), developed into a dynamic approach emphasizing company involvement in job programs.

6. Method: Installed by management.

7. Design: University- and company-trained groups were matched on demographic variables. Ratings of performance for the experimental groups
   were compared during training. Six months after completion of training, absenteeism and turnover rates were compared to those of normal
   hires.

8. Productivity Results: During training, the company-trained workers
   were rated somewhat higher on performance than were university-trained
   workers. Six months after training, the university-trained group had
   a significantly higher turnover rate than did either company-trained
   hires or normal hires; both trained groups had a significantly higher
   absenteeism rate than did normal hires, with the absenteeism rate of
   the university-trained group statistically higher than that of the
   company trained group.

9. Other Results: None reported.

10. Intervening Effects: None reported.

84

*11. Limitations: A. Absence of control group.
B. Company program unexpectedly turned out to be dynamic.
F. Small sample.

1. Reference: Rush, H.M.F. Job design for motivation. New York: The
   Conference Board, 1971, pp. 46-55.

2. Conclusions: Restructuring a job may not affect production rate, error
   rate, or job attitudes.*

3. Organization: U.S. Internal Revenue Service, Statistics of Income
   Program.

4. Workers: Tax examiners, 95% female; median age = 38 years; median education = 12th grade. N = 44, divided into four groups.

5. Program: The tax examiner's job was redesigned, using seven changes.
   These were (a) Direct contact between the verifier and the editor.
   (b) Verification by each unit of its own editing. (c) Rotation
   between editing and verifying. (d) "Specialization" of some editors
   in the returns of certain industries. (e) Broadening of scope by
   assignment of some working leaders to projects. (f) Weekly unit
   meetings. (g) Orientation of jobs to overall operation.

6. Method: Installed by management.

7. Design: Two experimental and two control groups were used. The use of
   the extra experimental and control groups was in order to take into
   account both the greater experience of the workers and the increased
   complexity of some jobs in these extra groups. Experimental and control subjects were matched on several variables. The results of the
   experiment were measured in terms of (a) Production rate (number of
   tax returns examined and edited per hour). (b) Error rate (the number
   of errors per return). (c) Job motivation (measured via a 16-item
   job-reaction questionnaire). This questionnaire was administered
   prior to the changes and again near the conclusion of the experiment.
   Results covered a six-month interval.

8. Productivity Results: In the first set of groups, examiners' production rates were significantly higher and error rates were significantly
   lower in the experimental than in the control group. In the second
   set, composed of more experienced workers doing more complex work,
   production rates were significantly lower in the experimental than in
   the control group; both the experimental and the control groups showed
   production rates that declined over the six-month interval; there were
   no significant differences and no changes in error rates between the
   experimental and control group. The combination of all results showed
   no overall differences in productivity between experimental and control groups.

85

9. Other Results: Before-and-after measures of job attitudes showed no differences in attitudes.

10. Intervening Effects: The production rate could have been affected by an increasingly complex workload, as well as by the time spent on developing specialists and on rotating workers between duties. Also, the job changes were described as trivial.

*11. Limitations: D. Trivial changes in job design.
                    E. Workers described as concerned with bread-and-butter conditions.
                    F. Small sample.

1. Reference: Rush, H.M.F. <u>Job design for motivation</u>. New York: The
   Conference Board, 1971, pp. 67-70.

2. Conclusions: In a continuous-process industry, incorporation of a
   lower-level cleaning job with another job may result in increased productivity of the former.*

3. Organization: PPG Industries, Fiber Glass Division, North Carolina;
   a continuous-process industry.

4. Workers: 92 twist-frame operators (transfer fiber from large tubes onto
   smaller bobbins); not unionized.

5. Program: Incorporation of frame-cleaning job with twist-frame operator
   job to increase utilization of manpower and machines. Program was
   first introduced by a trial run involving 10% of the total twist-frame
   operation. During subsequent weeks, the new procedure was installed in
   a larger percentage of the operation. Conversion of the entire
   operation occurred over a 10-week period.

6. Method: Installed by management.

7. Design: Before-and-after measurement of experimental group only.

8. Productivity Results: Productivity (not specified) increased 12% over
   the figures for the previous two years.

9. Other Results: None reported.

10. Intervening Effects: None reported.

*11. Limitations: A. Absence of control group.
                   C. Criteria not described in detail.
                   F. No tests of significance.

DOT: 355
SIC: I-805
Program: 3,7
Criterion: 2

1. Reference: Sard, P. & Berni, R. An incentive contract for nursing home aides. <u>American Journal of Nursing</u>, 1974, <u>74</u>, 475-477.

2. Conclusions: The behavior of nursing-home patients may be improved through a program of financial incentives both to the patients and to the aides, coupled with additional instruction of the aides.

3. Organization: Nursing home (Washington state).

4. Workers: Nursing home aides; 16 selected patients who were the most inactive.

5. Program: Instruction plus incentive pay: during each of three treatment weeks, 15-minute sessions with aides to explain techniques for increasing patient socialization and activity; for each improved patient at end of week, aides given $5 bonus to share among themselves; patients given $2 bonus if they increased their activity.

6. Method: Installed by management and consultants.

7. Design: 16 patients assigned randomly to either experimental or control group, 8 in each; time-series measures of activity recorded and averaged for each patient during randomized schedule for two weeks prior to treatment; for three weeks of treatment; and for two follow-up weeks beginning three weeks after the end of treatment.

8. Productivity Results: Five of eight patients in experimental group showed statistically significant improvement in activity; small, positive but insignificant changes in control group. Same results for follow-up observations.

9. Other Results: None reported.

10. Intervening Effects: None reported.

11. Limitations: E. Small and possibly unrepresentative sample.

1. Reference: Scheflen, K., Lawler, E.E. & Hackman, J.R. Long term impact
   of employee participation in the development of pay incentive plans: A
   field experiment revisited. Journal of Applied Psychology, 1971, 55,
   182-186.

2. Conclusions: When imposed by management, a monetary-incentive plan for
   good attendance was found to be less effective than one that had been
   adopted on the basis of worker participation. Discontinuation of the
   latter plan resulted in a deterioration of attendance.*

3. Organization: Small company providing building-maintenance services on
   a contract basis.

4. Workers: Part-time custodial workers; low educational level; mainly of
   minority groups; age ranges from 16 to over 70.

5. Program: Pay-incentive plan to reward attendance. Three work groups
   participated in developing a pay-incentive plan which was then implemented within these groups; the plan was also imposed by management
   on two other work groups. The program was later discontinued by
   management in two of the former three groups.

6. Method: Installed by management.

7. Design: Measures taken in two of the initial groups, before and after
   discontinuation of experimental program; comparison with the group that
   continued.

8. Productivity Results: Attendance decreased to below pre-treatment
   levels in the two groups where the participatively set program was discontinued, but not in the comparison group where the program remained
   in effect. In the two groups where the plan had been imposed, attendance gradually improved, although not to the level of the participative
   comparison group.

9. Other Results: At the end of one year, an increase in attendance was
   found in the groups where management imposed the incentive plan.

10. Intervening Effects: None reported.

*11. Limitations: B. Non-equivalence of comparison groups.
                   E. Part-time, low-skilled workers.

1. Reference: Schwartz, S. Decentralizing a community mental health
   center's service delivery system. Hospital and Community Psychiatry,
   1974, 25, 740-742.

2. Conclusions: Decentralization of services, plus integration of functions, may increase productivity.*

3. Organization: Hahnemann Community Mental Health Center in Philadelphia.

4. Workers: Five teams, each with about 12 full-time staff members and
   five students, and comprising psychiatrists, psychologists, psychiatric
   social workers, psychiatric nurses, and mental health workers.

5. Program: Reorganization featuring integration and decentralization:
   outpatient and emergency services were combined under new adult outpatient service, which was organized into five decentralized mental-
   health-sciences teams, each serving a sub-area; all directed by a
   medical and by an associate director; relocation from central into
   neighborhood facilities.

6. Method: Installed by management.

7. Design: Measures taken in experimental group only before and after reorganization.

8. Productivity Results: At end of two years, there was an increase of
   586 active cases and a 12.4% increase in proportion of cases deriving
   from catchment area; number of catchment-area outpatients admitted to
   inpatient care remained stable.

9. Other Results: Attitude survey after decentralization: 85% of staff
   preferred new structure.

10. Intervening Effects: None reported.

*11. Limitations: A. Absence of control group.
                   F. No tests of significance.

1. Reference: Seltzer, A., Moskowitz, A.S., Lucas, T. & Moskowitz, J.A.
   Welfare recipients as paraprofessionals: Utilization in facility for
   retarded parients. New York State Journal of Medicine, 1975, 75,
   751-755.
2. Conclusions: Preservice training of carefully selected welfare recipients improves retention after employment.*

3. Organization: A New York State institution for retarded patients
   (Willowbrook).

4. Workers: 187 unemployed welfare recipients selected as candidates for
   jobs in the state school. 85% of the candidates were black; ages
   ranged from 18 to 56 years.

5. Program: Selection and training. Candidates were selected after an
   intensive-stress interview and after their employment history and
   references were checked. Those selected then participated in a preservice training program, 50 hours over two weeks, consisting of
   didactic education and on-the-job observation. All candidates were
   guaranteed jobs either as assistant mental-hygiene-therapy aides or
   as hospital-care workers.

6. Method: Installed by management and consultants.

7. Design: Non-equivalent control group.

8. Productivity Results: The overall turnover rate was 15.8% for the
   trained group and 30-45% for an untrained group of workers.

9. Other Results: None reported.

10. Intervening Effects: None reported.

*11. Limitations: B. Non-equivalence of comparison groups.
                   F. No tests of significance.

1. Reference: Sisson, G.R. Development of training for a new manufacturing process. Training and Development Journal, 1971, 26(12), 22-31.

2. Conclusions: Cost savings and production benefits may be realized by
   developing a team-training program for a start-up process.*

3. Organization: Johns Manville Corporation, a process industry.

4. Workers: Crews who were to operate a new manufacturing process.

5. Program: Conversion from a consultant approach to team training. The
   training program was developed using a systems approach.

6. Method: Installed by management.

7. Design: Post-training measures of experimental groups only, compared
   to projections based on previous methods.

8. Productivity Results: At the end of 30 days, an average of 50,000 good
   production units were produced, exceeding the expected production of
   44,000 units; costs were significantly decreased; there was a 4.4%
   increase in budget efficiency. This was reported to represent a 175%
   return on training-dollar investment.

9. Other Results: The number of mechanical breakdowns normally occurring
   during startups was reported to have been lower than expected.

10. Intervening Effects: The new manufacturing equipment used was capable
    of increasing production by 50%, thus possibly accounting for the
    results.

*11. Limitations: A. Absence of control group.
                   D. Study limited to a particular type of manufacturing
                      operation.

1. Reference: Skuja, A.T., Schneidmuhl, A.M. & Mandell, W. Alcoholism counselor trainees: Some changes in job related functioning following training. Journal of Drug Education, 1975, 5, 151-157.

2. Conclusions: A training program for alcoholism counselors may improve their on-the-job performance ratings.*

3. Organization: Alcoholism Counselor Training Program of Johns Hopkins University School of Hygiene and Public Health, Baltimore, Maryland.

4. Workers: 41 trainees; average age 41 years; 13 women, nine blacks; all completed high school, six completed college, and three went beyond college; 15 were recovered alcoholics of two or more years; six worked in private agencies and 35 in government.

5. Program: Training program for paraprofessionals employed in agencies serving alcoholics: (a) 10-week in-residence phase of didactic lecture-discussions and experiential learning activities. (b) 17-week phase of on-the-job experience under regular supervision in employing agency.

6. Method: Installed by management.

7. Design: Before-and-after measurements of experimental group only, with evaluation by supervisor at end of Weeks 7 and 14 of second training phase.

8. Productivity Results: For most trainees, moderate positive changes in ratings of overall job performance and in four other performance ratings.

9. Other Results: None reported.

10. Intervening Effects: None reported.

*11. Limitations: A. Absence of control group.
                    C. Supervisor ratings; limited to training period.
                    F. No tests of significance.

DOT: 195   #93
SIC: J-944
Program: 14
Criterion: 1,2,3,6,7

1. Reference: Spiegel, A.H., III. How outsiders overhauled a public
   agency. Harvard Business Review, 1975, 53(1), 116-124. (See also
   Abstract No. 34.)

2. Conclusions: Overhaul of the New York City welfare administration was
   followed by improved productivity and by cost reduction.*

3. Organization: New York City's Human Resources (welfare) Administration.

4. Workers: 27,000-man agency with about 600 managers; industrial
   engineers and specialists hired during overhaul period.

5. Program: System overhaul, including automation; revamping of welfare-
   center operations; tightening of management controls and account-
   ability; and replacement of incompetent managers.

6. Method: Installed by management.

7. Design: Before-and-after measures of experimental cases only.

8. Productivity Results: Error rate reduced by about half; 30% reduction
   in lateness rate; 29% reduction in absenteeism. 16% increase in staff
   productivity. Caseload reduction of 109,000 people. $200 million
   savings in welfare payments.

9. Other Results: None reported.

10. Intervening Effects. None reported.

*11. Limitations: A. Absence of control group.
                    E. Started with mismanaged operation.

155

1. Reference: Stansbury, W.M. Reducing clerical turnover. <u>Personnel
   Journal</u>, 1973, <u>52</u>, 209-212.

2. Conclusions: Turnover was reduced following a number of changes in the
   work system.*

3. Organization: Blue Cross-Blue Shield, Topeka, Kansas.

4. Workers: All non-exempt clerical employees of company; number unspecified.

5. Program: Introduction of 13 new programs or operational changes:
   (a) Employee orientation. (b) Post-employment interview. (c) Employee
   counseling. (d) Medical training. (e) Supervisor counseling. (f)
   supervisor training. (g) Testing (subsequently eliminated). (h) Job
   evaluation. (i) Industrial nurse on premises. (j) Performance evaluation. (k) Management training. (l) Job enlargement. (m) Electronic
   data processing.

6. Method: Installed by management.

7. Design: Before-and-after measures, using a single case.

8. Productivity Results: After changes were introduced, turnover decreased
   21.1%.

9. Other Results: Morale said to increase after introduction of programs.

10. Intervening Effects: None reported.

*11. Limitations: Because of lack of specificity, the following defects may
    apply--A. Absence of control group.
             F. No tests of significance.

DOT: unspecified   #95
SIC: D-unspecified
Program: 13
Criterion: 1,3,5,6,7

1. Reference: Steward, G.V. & Larsen, J.M. A four-day, three-day per
   week application to a continuous-production operation. _Management of
   Personnel Quarterly_, 1971, 10, 13-20.

2. Conclusions: Production may be increased through a change in the work
   schedule to a four-day, three-day schedule. The effect may largely be
   due to increased number of man-hours worked, reflected in increased
   payroll.*

3. Organization: Small manufacturing company in the Southeast.

4. Workers: All personnel in one department of the firm.

5. Program: For three months, conversion to alternate four-day and three-
   day workweeks, repeating two-week cycles.

6. Method: Installed by management.

7. Design: Before-and-after measures, using experimental group only.

8. Productivity Results: At the end of three months, in comparison with
   the previous work-schedule, average monthly production-output increased 27%; productivity (monthly output divided by total number
   man-hours worked) increased 3.1%; turnover remained unchanged; tardiness decreased 6.9%; and absenteeism increased 4.9%.

9. Other Results: Average total monthly payroll increased 15%; overtime
   costs decreased 4.9%.

10. Intervening Effects: Total employment increased 62%; hours worked
    increased 22%.

*11. Limitations: A. Absence of control group.
                   E. Limited to a continuous-production operation.
                   F. Small sample.
                      No tests of significance.

157

1. Reference: Stude, E.W. Evaluation of short-term training for rehabilitation counselors: Effectiveness of an institute on epilepsy. Rehabilitation Counseling Bulletin, 1973, 16, 146-154.

2. Conclusions: Short-term training, even if effective in imparting information to counselors, may not produce more positive attitudes or increase counseling effectiveness.

3. Organization: California State Department of Rehabilitation.

4. Workers: 180 rehabilitation counselors.

5. Program: Two-day training program which provided counselors with
   specific information about epilepsy and encouraged them to apply this
   information to the vocational rehabilitation of persons with epilepsy.

6. Method: Installed by management.

7. Design: Counselors were randomly selected and randomly assigned to an
   experimental group and two control groups. One control group attended
   another institute, while the second control group did not receive any
   training. Measures of attitudes and of job performance were taken five
   months after the experimental treatment.

8. Productivity Results: The quality of job performance of rehabilitation
   counselors with their epileptic clients, as measured by changes in
   clients' status, did not significantly change during the five-month
   period after completion of training.

9. Other Results: See below.

10. Intervening Effects: Trained counselors acquired more information, but
    did not exhibit more positive attitudes toward epileptics.

11. Limitations: C. Changes in case status over limited duration may be
                  insensitive indicator.

1. Reference: Tjersland, T. <u>Changing worker behavior</u> (DLMA-82-36-71-02-1).
   New York: Manpower Laboratory, American Telephone and Telegraph,
   December 1972. (NTIS No. PB-221 074.)

2. Conclusions: The rewarding of perfect attendance by giving time off or
   supplemental pay produced a net improvement in attendance, accompanied
   by a small increase in tardiness. However, the program cost slightly
   more than it saved, mainly because of the relatively small number with
   poor attendance records.*

3. Organization: Human Resource Center established by Pacific Telephone
   and Telegraph in conjunction with the Manpower Laboratory of American
   Telephone and Telegraph.

4. Workers: 162 employees in the Traffic Department of the Southwest
   District.

5. Program: An awards program was instituted to increase attendance.
   Employees earned one half-day off with pay for each period of 25
   consecutive schedule days of perfect attendance. Employees were
   allowed to take supplemental pay in lieu of time off. In the span of a
   year, an employee with perfect attendance would earn 10 awards; this
   totaled a week's paid vacation or a week's extra pay.

6. Method: Installed by management.

7. Design: Comparison of attendance data of experimental group for the
   three months prior to initiation of program and for the three months
   afterwards.

8. Productivity Results: After implementation of the program, the average
   rate of "incidental" absences (six or less days of consecutive absence)
   decreased from 1.88 days to 1.43 days. There was a 9% increase in
   perfect attendance and a 3.5% decrease in poor attendance. 88.5% of
   the 24 employees classified as "poor" in attendance showed improvement;
   37% of all the employees in the department showed improvement and 25%
   showed a worsening of attendance rates. There was an insignificant
   decrease in number of times absent, as well as a small increase both in
   the number of times tardy and in the average total minutes of tardiness.

9. Other Results: A cost-benefit analysis revealed that the program ran
   at a small net loss per month during the period of study.

10. Intervening Effects: None reported.

*11. Limitations: A. Absence of control group.
                   D. Short-term study (three months).
                   F. No tests of significance.

1. Reference: Tushman, M. <u>Organizational change: An exploratory study and case history</u>. Ithaca: New York State School of Industrial and Labor Relations, Cornell University, 1974.

2. Conclusions: Productivity may improve as a result of extensive changes emphasizing ideological, structural and behavioral modifications.*

3. Organization: Becket, a glass-production plant.

4. Workers: Plant manager, and staff of the engineering and manufacturing areas.

5. Program: Planned organizational change emphasizing three aspects:
   (a) Ideological change: changes in values, norms, expectations, and criteria for success, as defined and practiced by top management.
   (b) Structural change: changes in authority distribution, communication flow, control systems, decision-making level, and work flow.
   (c) Behavioral change: reeducation of behavioral knowledge and skills (new language norms and values) obtained from a packaged organizational development program (Blake and Mouton's Managerial Grid). The changes were traced over a 42-month period.

6. Method: Installed by top management.

7. Design: Measures in experimental case only.

8. Productivity Results: Productivity (measured in dollars per man-hour) rose from $7.80 to $10.38 in approximately one year.

9. Other Results: The gross margin figure increased by 12.8% compared to 1.8% the previous year.

10. Intervening Effects: Massive changes in structural and behavioral variables were reported to have taken place during the period.

*11. Limitations: A. Absence of control group.
                   F. No tests of significance.

DOT: 520
SIC: D-204
Program: 14
Criterion: 2,3,6

1. Reference: Walton, R.E. How to counter alienation in the plant.
   Harvard Business Review, 1972, 50(6), 70-81. (For a later report of
   this project, see Abstract No. 47.)

2. Conclusions: A markedly changed work system as installed in a new
   plant is reported to have resulted in many improvements in performance,
   as compared to performance in an old plant.*

3. Organization: Pet-food manufacturing plant.

4. Workers: Operators who staffed a new manufacturing facility.

5. Program: Nine key features were cited in the organizational design of
   the new plant: (a) Autonomous work groups. (b) Functions like maintenance and quality control, typically performed by support now the
   responsibility of each team. (c) Challenging job assignments
   (avoidance of assignment of only menial duties to personnel). (d) Job
   mobility, and team members paid for learning more aspects of the total
   manufacturing system. (e) Team leaders, chosen from foreman level,
   responsible for team development and group decision making. (f) Production decisions, formerly made by supervisors, now made at operator
   level. (g) No preplanned rules for governing the plant community.
   (h) Minimization of differential status symbols. (i) In light of
   experience, continuous reassessment of the plant's productivity and
   its impact on employee concerns.

6. Method: Initiated by management, with worker participation.

7. Design: Case study. Post-installation data from the new plant were
   compared with figures for an old non-equivalent plant and with industry
   norms.

8. Productivity Results: After 18 months in operation of the new plant,
   the fixed overhead rate was 33% lower than in the old plant. Quality
   rejects were 92% lower. Absenteeism was calculated to be 9% below the
   industry norm. Annual savings were reported to be $600,000. Turnover
   was reported to be below the industry average, and the safety record
   was said to be one of the best in the company.

9. Other Results: Employees were said to derive satisfaction from their
   jobs.

10. Intervening Effects: New equipment was reported to be responsible for
    some of these results. Effects were believed to be mainly due to
    reduced alienation of workers.

*11. Limitations: B. Non-equivalence of comparison groups.
                   E. Highly selective and newly recruited work force.
                   F. No tests of significance.

DOT: 235
SIC: E-481
Program: 1,3
Criterion: 5   #100

1. Reference: Wanous, J. Effects of a realistic job preview on job
   acceptance, job attitudes and job survival. Journal of Applied Psychology, 1973, 58, 327-332.

2. Conclusions: Initial job expectations may be reduced by showing a
   realistic job-preview film, but there may not be significant effects
   on job acceptance or on later retention.

3. Organization: Telephone company located in the East.

4. Workers: 80 female new hires for job of phone-operator.

5. Program: Effect on prospective hires of realistic job preview (a
   realistic film emphasizing both good and bad aspects of the job) vs.
   traditional job preview (a film emphasizing good aspects of the job
   only).

6. Method: Installed by management.

7. Design: Random assignment of subjects to view either a realistic or a
   traditional job-preview film.

8. Productivity Results: After three months, job survival did not differ
   significantly between the two groups.

9. Other Results: Rate of job acceptance was not affected. Realistic-
   job-preview group had fewer thoughts of quitting.

10. Intervening Effects: Job expectations were lower after realistic than
    after traditional preview.

11. Limitations: C. Limited duration of measurements.
                  E. Unemployment level increased during study; subjects
                     volunteered for study.

1. Reference: Weed, E., Jr. Job enrichment "cleans up" at Texas Instruments. In J.R. Maher (ed.), <u>New perspectives in job enrichment</u>. New York: Van Nostrand, Reinhold Co., 1971, pp. 55-75. (See also Rush, H.M.F. <u>Job design for motivation</u>. New York: The Conference Board, 1971, pp. 39-45.)

2. Conclusions: An extensive set of changes in the work system was followed by improved performance, reduced turnover, and cost savings. Although cited as a case of job enrichment, many other elements were also changed.*

3. Organization: Texas Instruments, Dallas, Texas.

4. Workers: Four exempt supervisors; eight working foremen; 75 cleaning personnel (50 men, 25 women). Average educational level of the cleaning personnel was between fourth and fifth grade.

5. Program: Attempted to improve the overall cleanliness level through a procedure involving cleaning-services training for exempt supervisors, and orientation programs for working foremen and cleaning personnel. The program included development of teamwork in groups, and the identification of organizational goals and of the elements in attainment of these goals. Adjunct programs included new-employee orientation and training, a quarterly orientation program, work-simplification training, and weekly team meetings. A pay raise from $1.40 to $1.80 per hour was given.

6. Method: Installed by management.

7. Design: Before-and-after measures with the experimental group only.

8. Productivity Results: The cleanliness-level rating improved from 65% to 85%. Quarterly turnover declined from 100% to 9.8%. Annual cost savings realized was $103,000.

9. Other Results: None reported.

10. Intervening Effects: None reported.

*11. Limitations: A. Absence of control group.
                              C. Rating criterion may be affected by rater's knowledge of program.
                              F. Basically a single case.

DOT: 187
SIC: I-806
Program: 3,6,10
Criterion: 2,6,15

1. Reference: Wexley, K.N. & Nemeroff, W.F. Effectiveness of positive reinforcement and goal setting as methods of management development. Journal of Applied Psychology, 1975, 60, 446-450.

2. Conclusions: Managerial groups trained to be more considerate of employees through programs involving role playing, appraisal, and goal setting significantly reduce their subordinates' rate of absenteeism. The addition of telecoaching did not improve the results.

3. Organization: Nine departments of a large urban medical center, including nursing, medical records, credit, maintenance, and various other services.

4. Workers: 27 managers, nearly all first-level supervisors; five male and 22 female; median age 43.5 years; median experience as managers 9.5 years. 114 subordinates completed questionnaires; average twelfth-grade education and nine-year tenure.

5. Program: Two managerial-development programs designed to improve managers' behavior (Consideration/Integration) and their subordinates' absenteeism and satisfaction. Both programs involved five role-playing exercises; appraisal and goal setting took place during and after the workshop (the trainer reinforced behaviors and assigned specific goals). One of the programs also included telecoaching, a behavior-modification technique in which the trainer, during the role-playing exercises, reinforces and shapes trainee behavior by giving immediate verbal feedback through an ear device.

6. Method: Installed by management and consultants.

7. Design: Post-test-only control-group design, with measures taken 60 days after completion of training; nine managers (randomly assigned by department) in each of the two training groups and in the one control group.

8. Productivity Results: Subordinate absenteeism was significantly lower in the two training groups than in the control group. The two training groups did not differ significantly from each other in any of the measures.

9. Other Results: Subordinate work satisfaction was significantly higher in the group trained without telecoaching; the telecoached and control groups showed no difference in work satisfaction.

10. Intervening Effects: The two training groups scored significantly higher than the control group on the Consideration and Integration scales of the Leader Behavior Description Questionnaire filled out by their subordinates.

11. Limitations: C. Short-term period of measurement.
                   E. Small and possibly unrepresentative sample.

1. Reference: Yukl, G.A. & Latham, G.P. Consequences of reinforcement schedules and incentive magnitudes for employee performance: Problems encountered in an industrial setting. Journal of Applied Psychology, 1975, 60, 294-298.

2. Conclusions: Incentive pay awarded in direct proportion to output has greater effect than when awarded on a partially variable basis--perhaps, in part, as a result of practical problems in implementing the latter system of awards.

3. Organization: Logging company.

4. Workers: Four seed-planting crews in North Carolina; primarily young, uneducated black males and females; marginal workers, with productivity, turnover, and absenteeism unacceptable to management.

5. Program: Three reinforcement conditions: (a) Continuous schedule of reinforcement (CRF), with, in addition to $2 hourly pay, a $2 incentive for planting each bag of seed. (b) Variable-ratio schedule (VR2), with a $4 incentive for planting a bag of seed and guessing correct outcome of one coin toss. (c) Variable-ratio (VR4), with an $8 incentive for planting a bag of seed and guessing outcome of two coin tosses.

6. Method: Installed by management and consultants.

7. Design: Random assignment of one crew to each of the three experimental conditions (N = 13 in CRF, 14 in VR2, and 11 in VR4). A fourth group (for comparison) was geographically isolated. Crew performance-measures were collected for the three-week period before the experiment, and for the period from nine to 15 weeks afterward.

8. Productivity Results: Continuous reinforcement schedule produced a 33% increase in output, compared to an 18% increase in VR4 and to small declines in VR2 and in the comparison group; the three experimental groups significantly differed from one another. There was also a significant difference in absolute levels of output among the three conditions, with CRF performance significantly higher than VR2, and VR4 not significantly different from other two conditions. CRF was described as "highly effective" as far as cost/effectiveness ratio was concerned.

9. Other Results: None reported.

10. Intervening Effects: None reported.

11. Limitations: B. Non-equivalence of groups.
                 C. Period of measurement was rather short.
                 D. Among some workers, incentive procedures created
                    confusion, complications, and negative reactions.
                    VR was not pure variable ratio, since it was incre-
                    mental to hourly pay.
                 E. Under variable ratio, some female workers and one
                    supervisor disapproved of what they felt was
                    gambling. The socio-economic and cultural back-
                    ground of the workers may have been a factor.
                    Small sample.

SECTION III

APPENDIX
and
INDEXES

APPENDIX

SOURCES OF LITERATURE SEARCH

As part of our search process, we read <u>Psychological Abstracts</u>, <u>Personnel Management Abstracts</u>, and <u>Sociological Abstracts</u>. These journals draw material from a comprehensive list of scientific, medical, technical, and business journals published both in the United States and abroad; books; and monographs.

In addition to our research in the three abstract journals, a search was made of the following individual journals during the years 1971-1975:

Academy of Management Journal

Administrative Science Quarterly

Industrial Engineering

Journal of Applied Behavior Analysis

Journal of Applied Behavioral Science

Journal of Applied Psychology

Personnel

Personnel Administrator

Personnel Journal

Personnel Psychology

Training and Development Journal

INDEXES

A. PROGRAM INDEX

The experimental changes that the various studies made were classified
into fourteen categories. These represent the programs or "action levers"
by which the experimenters hoped to improve productivity. Under each of
these fourteen rubrics, given below, we list the abstract numbers of the
studies employing that program, either alone or in combination with other
programs. This list, therefore, serves as an index for the reader interested in locating studies dealing with a particular type of program, such
as training and instruction, organizational structure, and so forth.

1. Selection and placement. Abstracts 20, 52, 90, 100.

2. Job development and promotion. None.

3. Training and instruction. Abstracts 1, 2, 3, 4, 6, 12, 13, 17, 18, 19,
    27, 28, 32, 33, 38, 46, 59, 62, 65, 66, 67, 69, 70, 72, 78, 79, 80, 82,
    83, 84, 87, 90, 91, 92, 96, 100, 102.

4. Appraisal and feedback. Abstracts 1, 3, 5, 18, 21, 36, 48, 67, 69.

5. Management by objectives. Abstracts 18, 40.

6. Goal setting. Abstracts 48, 54, 55, 56, 57, 75, 79, 102.

7. Financial compensation. Abstracts 9, 39, 71, 73, 74, 75, 87, 88, 97,
    103.

8. Job design. Abstracts 7, 13, 14, 16, 22, 25, 37, 42, 43, 44, 50, 51,
    60, 64, 81, 85, 86.

9. Group design. Abstracts 22, 23, 26, 30.

10. Supervisory methods. Abstracts 5, 8, 11, 13, 28, 32, 33, 36, 38, 59,
    76, 78, 102.

11. Organizational structure. Abstracts 45, 58, 59, 88, 89.

175.

12. **Physical working conditions**. None.

13. **Work schedule**. Abstracts 9, 10, 29, 53, 63, 68, 95, 97.

14. **Socio-technical system**. Abstracts 11, 15, 24, 34, 35, 47, 49, 61, 77, 93, 94, 98, 99, 101.

B. CRITERION INDEX

Potential productivity outcomes or criteria were classified into fifteen categories. These represent the dependent variables by which the results may be assessed. Studies are listed below for each criterion by abstract number. This index is for the reader interested in locating studies dealing with a specific outcome, such as production quality, turnover, and so forth.

1. **Production quantity**. Abstracts 1, 7, 8, 9, 10, 11, 14, 15, 22, 24, 25, 26, 28, 31, 34, 38, 40, 42, 44, 45, 46, 47, 49, 50, 51, 53, 54, 55, 56, 57, 58, 59, 62, 63, 66, 73, 75, 76, 77, 78, 79, 81, 85, 86, 89, 91, 93, 95, 103.

2. **Production quality**. Abstracts 1, 3, 6, 7, 11, 12, 14, 15, 16, 17, 18, 22, 23, 25, 26, 30, 32, 33, 34, 36, 37, 38, 40, 41, 42, 43, 44, 46, 48, 49, 51, 52, 58, 60, 63, 64, 65, 66, 67, 70, 72, 74, 84, 85, 87, 92, 93, 96, 99, 101, 102.

3. **Production costs**. Abstracts 1, 2, 5, 8, 13, 14, 15, 19, 24, 25, 29, 34, 37, 39, 44, 47, 48, 49, 51, 58, 59, 61, 64, 81, 91, 93, 95, 97, 98, 99, 101.

4. **Job success or progress**. Abstracts 4, 6, 52, 82.

5. **Turnover**. Abstracts 13, 19, 20, 22, 26, 27, 29, 35, 43, 44, 47, 51, 55, 61, 63, 69, 80, 83, 84, 90, 94, 95, 100, 101.

6. **Absenteeism**. Abstracts 2, 8, 13, 22, 23, 24, 26, 29, 30, 31, 35, 39, 40, 41, 44, 47, 48, 50, 55, 61, 68, 71, 76, 84, 88, 93, 95, 97, 99, 102.

7. **Tardiness**. Abstracts 21, 24, 71, 93, 95, 97.

8. **Job refusal**. Abstract 20.

176

9. <u>Accidents</u>. Abstracts 2, 47, 48, 55.   4

10. <u>Strikes</u>. None.   0

11. <u>Slowdowns</u>. None.   0

12. <u>Grievances</u>. Abstracts 2, 15, 40, 58.   4

13. <u>Alcoholism and drug abuse</u>. None.   0

14. <u>Disciplinary actions</u>. Abstract 2.   1

15. <u>Attitudes</u>. Abstracts 1, 7, 14, 15, 18, 23, 29, 30, 35, 41, 44, 47, 48, 52, 57, 68, 76, 85, 102.   19

C. OCCUPATIONAL INDEX

Some readers may be interested in locating studies dealing with a particular occupation. For this purpose, we have identified on each abstract the occupational classification(s) of the workers involved. We have employed the two-digit code supplied by the <u>Dictionary of Occupational Titles</u> (DOT), assigning the code as best we could on the basis of information furnished in the report. The present index lists the DOT code numbers in sequence and, next to each, the numbers of the corresponding abstracts. For convenience, the DOT categories are presented at the end of this index.

0,1 Professional, technical, and managerial.
    <u>04</u>: 67, 89, 92.
    <u>07</u>: 9, 18, 31, 46, 79, 89.
    <u>09</u>: 3.
    <u>16</u>: 21, 66, 85.
    <u>18</u>: 4, 13, 19, 28, 29, 31, 32, 33, 35, 36, 38, 47, 49, 59, 62, 78.
    <u>19</u>: 31, 34, 89.

2 Clerical and sales.
  20: 14, 21, 22, 31, 42, 57, 64, 94.
  21: 16, 43, 44, 81.
  23: 100.
  24: 6, 23, 35, 45, 51.
  26: 52.
  27: 52.
  28: 40, 52.
  29: 59.
  2(unspecified): 53, 81, 83.

3 Service.
  31: 13.
  35: 12, 65, 70, 74, 75, 79, 87, 90.
  36: 8.
  37: 17, 37, 72.
  38: 48, 83, 88, 101.

5 Processing.
  50: 1.
  52: 47, 99.
  59: 91.

6 Machine trades.
  63: 48.
  68: 50, 86.

7 Bench work.
  70: 7.
  71: 61.
  72: 25, 26, 40, 60.
  77: 98.
  78: 10, 20.
  7(unspecified): 27, 39, 52, 58, 71, 77.

8 Structural.
  80: 2, 15, 49, 58.
  82: 41, 76, 80.
  86: 76, 82.

9 Miscellaneous.
  94: 54, 55, 56, 103.

Unspecified. (author's category)
5, 11, 24, 29, 63, 68, 84, 95, 97.

The code numbers in this index correspond to the Dictionary of Occupational Titles (DOT) categories that appear on the following pages.

DICTIONARY OF OCCUPATIONAL TITLES

(Volume II. <u>Occupational Classification and Industry Index</u>,
United States Department of Labor, 1965, 3rd edition)

0,1 - PROFESSIONAL, TECHNICAL, AND MANAGERIAL OCCUPATIONS

04 Occupations in life sciences

07 Occupations in medicine and health

09 Occupations in education

16 Occupations in administrative specializations

18 Managers and officials, not elsewhere classified (n.e.c.)

19 Miscellaneous professional, technical, and managerial occupations

2 - CLERICAL AND SALES OCCUPATIONS

20 Stenography, typing, filing and related occupations

21 Computing and account-recording occupations

23 Information and message distribution occupations

24 Miscellaneous clerical occupations

26⎤
27⎬ Salesmen and salespersons, commodities
28⎦

29 Merchandising occupations, except salesmen

3 - SERVICE OCCUPATIONS

31 Food and beverage preparation and service occupations

35 Miscellaneous personal service occupations

36 Apparel and furnishings service occupations

37 Protective service occupations

38 Building and related service occupations

5 - PROCESSING OCCUPATIONS

50 Occupations in processing of metal

52 Occupations in processing of food, tobacco, and related products

59 Processing occupations, n.e.c.

6 - MACHINE TRADES OCCUPATIONS

63 Mechanics and machinery repairmen

68 Textile occupations

7 - BENCH WORK OCCUPATIONS

70 Occupations in fabrication, assembly, and repair of metal products, n.e.c.

71 Occupations in fabrication and repair of scientific and medical apparatus, photographic and optical goods, watches and clocks, and related products

72 Occupations in assembly and repair of electrical equipment

77 Occupations in fabrication and repair of sand, stone, clay, and glass products

78 Occupations in fabrication and repair of textile, leather, and related products

8 - STRUCTURAL WORK OCCUPATIONS

80 Occupations in metal fabricating, n.e.c.

82 Electrical assembling, installing, and repairing occupations

86 Construction occupations, n.e.c.

94 Occupations in logging

D. INDUSTRY INDEX

Some readers may be interested in locating studies performed in particular types of organizations. For this purpose, we have identified on each
abstract the type of organization involved. We have employed the United
States Standard Industrial Code (SIC), assigning the code as best we could on
the basis of information furnished in the report. The present index lists
the SIC code numbers in sequence and, next to each, the numbers of the corresponding abstracts. For convenience, at the end of this index are presented
the SIC categories--down to two digits, which is as far as we have refined
the classification.

A (1-9) Agriculture, forestry, and fishing.
  08: 35, 54, 55, 56, 57, 103.

D (20-39) Manufacturing.
  20: 47, 99.
  23: 10, 20.
  28: 39, 62, 68.
  32: 24, 83, 98.
  33: 1, 32, 33.
  35: 39, 41, 80.
  36: 11, 25, 26, 40, 60, 103.
  37: 2, 15, 49, 58.
  38: 39, 61.
  39: 39, 50.
  D(unspecified): 28, 52, 58, 71, 77, 91, 95.

E (40-49) Transportation, communications, electric, gas and sanitary
  services.
  41: 53, 76.
  42: 38.
  45: 5.
  48: 16, 19, 22, 42, 43, 45, 48, 97, 100.
  49: 84.
  E(unspecified): 83.

G (52-59) Retail trade.
   54: 59.

H (60-67) Finance, insurance, and real estate.
   60: 14, 23, 51, 64.
   63: 6, 44, 63, 87, 94.

I (70-89) Services.
   72: 8.
   79: 73.
   80: 9, 12, 13, 18, 21, 31, 46, 65, 70, 74, 79, 87.
   82: 3, 36.
   83: 7, 67, 75, 82.

J (91-97) Public administration.
   91: 30.
   92: 17.
   93: 66, 78, 85.
   94: 93.
   97: 37, 72.

Unspecified. (author's category)
4, 27, 29, 69.

STANDARD INDUSTRIAL CLASSIFICATION

(United States Office of Management and Budget,
Statistical Policy Division, 1972)

DIVISION A. AGRICULTURE, FORESTRY, AND FISHING

Major Group 08. Forestry

DIVISION D. MANUFACTURING

Major Group 20. Food and kindred products

Major Group 23. Apparel and other finished products made from fabrics and
                 similar materials

Major Group 28. Chemicals and allied products

Major Group 32. Stone, clay, glass, and concrete products

Major Group 33. Primary metal industries

182

Major Group 35. Machinery, except electrical

Major Group 36. Electrical and electronic machinery, equipment and supplies

Major Group 37. Transportation equipment

Major Group 38. Measuring, analyzing, and controlling instruments; photo-graphic medical and optical goods; watches and clocks

Major Group 39. Miscellaneous manufacturing industries

DIVISION E. TRANSPORTATION, COMMUNICATIONS, ELECTRIC, GAS, AND SANITARY SERVICES

Major Group 41. Local and suburban transit and interurban highway passenger transportation

Major Group 42. Motor freight transportation and warehousing

Major Group 45. Transportation by air

Major Group 48. Communications

Major Group 49. Electric, gas, and sanitary services

DIVISION G. RETAIL TRADE

Major Group 54. Food stores

DIVISION H. FINANCE, INSURANCE, AND REAL ESTATE

Major Group 60. Banking

Major Group 63. Insurance

DIVISION I. SERVICES

Major Group 72. Personal services

Major Group 79. Amusement and recreation services, except motion pictures

Major Group 80. Health services

Major Group 82. Educational services

Major Group 83. Social services

DIVISION J. PUBLIC ADMINISTRATION

Major Group 91. Executive, legislative, and general government, except finance

Major Group 92. Justice, public order, and safety

Major Group 94. Administration of human resources programs

Major Group 97. National security and international affairs

E. AUTHOR INDEX
(numbers refer to abstracts)

184

185